It's Not Where You Start, It's Where You Finish:

How I Won My Race from Last Place!

Live by choice

2nd edition

not by chance!

Dr. Michael Miller

It's Not Where You Start, It's Where You Finish:
How I Won My Race from Last Place!
Copyright © 2006 by Michael L. Miller
and Empowerment Press Publishing Company
All rights reserved

Published by: Empowerment Press Publishing Company
Printed in Canada

Book Design by Effectual Designs
Photo by Choice 1 Media
Editorial Director, Andria Cole

Books are available at special discounts for bulk purchases, sales promotion, fund raising, or educational purposes.

ISBN Number 13#: 978-0-9786263-8-9

ISBN Number 10#: 0-9786263-8-9

For more information write to:
Empowerment Press Publishing Company
PO Box 794,
Ellicott City, MD 21041-794
USA
www.apromisetopersevere.com

Dedication

The story that follows—all its love, hurt, and inspiration—is dedicated to my parents: The late Dennie Miller who is responsible for all I am and my mother, Nellie Miller, who has waited ever so patiently for my redemption while being gravely ill. Just recently, she told me, "Michael hurry up and write that book. I don't care if I die the day after you finished it. As long as I live to read the final page, my living will not be in vain."

No mama, it won't.

These pages are also dedicated to the single parents of the world and to all of America and Africa's troubled youth trying to overcome life's hurdles and challenges:

Here comes the sun!... brighter days are sure to come!

Acknowledgements

If life is a race, then there must be a coach to help one along the journey. I am fortunate to have been blessed with a variety of coaches who have walked with, supported, or carried me some measure of the way. Many wonderful and powerful people worked to make this project successful, and while it is possible to list each of them, space obligates me to identify only a few and to seek the forgiveness of the many others whose significant names are omitted.

I am humbled daily by God's graciousness and wisdom and particularly by his decision to make me a vessel of change that works to transform the lives of others. Thank you, God, for "ordering my steps." I also respectfully acknowledge those ancestors who fought and died so that I might pursue an education—thank you for guaranteeing my very existence.

And, to my parents, the late Dennie Miller and still-present Nellie Miller, who did the best they could with what they had. Mama, I apologize for all of the times you had to visit the school on account of my behavior, for all of the pain, the headaches, the trials, and tribulations. I hope this is no longer the case, and that, finally, I have given you peace. Daddy, your spirit will always be with me. I apologize for crashing the car—I'll pay you back when I meet you in Heaven. It is because of you I was prepared to follow my dreams. Thank you for giving me the tools I needed to beat the odds.

I am eternally grateful for the support of my children— Dévon, Destiny, and Brianna, who inspire me to take on the task of empowering people to empower themselves. Thank you for being so patient with Daddy, for always bringing sunshine and laughter into my life, and for reminding me why I do what I do. Thanks for giving me the time and space needed to write this book. Thank you for focusing my life and for making it complete and meaningful.

I want to especially express my deepest appreciation and gratitude for those who have stood with me since the beginning: the late Harlow Fullwood, Master Eddie Butcher, Grandmaster L.R. Butcher, and Walter Farrar for their encouragement and helping me to engage in the true essence of success through the power of discipline. Mrs. Beverley Arah, a phenomenal, selfless woman with a spirit big as heaven, for consistently and whole-heartedly encouraging me before and during this experience; even though I was "just a G.E.D. student." To my G.E.D. teacher and mentor, Mr. Jonathan White, for picking me up when I had fallen to an unimaginable low. Dr. Tonya Ringgold for her powerful words of wisdom, leadership, guidance and support. Thanks for continuing to push me beyond my measures.

A failing thank you to Oprah Winfrey—for these words lack the gratitude necessary to express just how much your benevolent support has mattered in my life. Thank you for assuming the financial responsibility of my academic matriculation to Morehouse College. Thank you for the enduring words of encouragement you bestow upon your viewing audience daily. It is because of you that so many of us are able to "Beat the Odds."

Though there are many, I sincerely want to thank a few Morehouse Men who have made it all possible for me to attend Morehouse College. I want to personally thank my Morehouse Brother Jim Henry, President of the D.C. Morehouse Alumni

Chapter for making the Oprah Winfrey scholarship connection possible. And most of all, I offer sincere gratitude to Dean Sterling Hudson for looking beyond my past faults and failures and for giving me a chance to be considered among the most elite Brothers that any academic institution in the world has to offer — to be a Morehouse Man. Thank you for making it all possible. I also want to personally thank my good friend and mentor, Dr. Ben Carson for encouraging and inspiring to me to "Think Big."

To my siblings (Sandra, Jeffrey, Donell, Dennie, Towanda, Kelly, Sheila, and Ronnie): Thank you for your companionship and support, and for sharing this wonderful life with me. Our history and love bind us forever. Special thanks to my big brother, mentor, and confidant, Dennie Jr.: Thanks for being you.

To my surrogate mom, Carol Kellam, for being everything one wishes a mother to be—patient, compassionate, and withstanding. Sorry for crashing your car though! To my sis Nita: Well, what can I say? I thank you, from way deep inside, for everything you have done for me. You are all a brother could need.

I also thank my editorial consultant, Andria Cole, for her continuous support. Okay Andria, it's done. We can stop fighting now. What a tedious process it has been. Sorry for being such a pain in the neck. You should have known I was going to be a pain from day one! Once again, thanks for all of the aforementioned coaches, for this book would not be without the support and aid of you.

Contents

Foreword:

by Dr. Ben Carson

At the 1908 Olympic Games held in London England, the Bishop of Central Pennsylvania, Ethelbert Talbot, gave a speech that has appeared on the scoreboard during Opening Ceremony at every modern Olympic event. Baron de Coubertin, a French pedagogue best known for founding the Olympic Games, was later inspired to adopt and quote the Olympic Creed. It stated, "The most important thing in the Olympic Games is not to win, but to take part just as the most important thing in life is not the triumph, but the struggle. The essential thing is not to have conquered, but to have fought well." Michael Miller's life is a testament of faith and perseverance to remind us just like in the Olympics, winning is not the most important thing; it is the eventual challenge for which we all struggle as we attempt to succeed.

Today, we face a frightening emergency with an unprecedented statistic in play. The average person in America lives to be about 80 years old. The first 20-25 of these years are spent one of two ways: Either the individual prepares educationally

1

or he or she does not. Those who prepare will likely spend the next 50-60 years reaping the many benefits of this groundwork; those who don't may spend those 5-6 decades suffering the consequences of this failure to plan. Life is a series of occurrences, but on every stage we choose and become responsible for the choices we make. Paul Harvey, a nationally acclaimed journalist and radio presenter said, "The secret of success is to get up when you fall down." Michael Miller, a former juvenile delinquent, street thug and high school dropout who became a father at the age of 14, certainly mirrors these facts. It wasn't until he was twenty-five years old that he joined the race. Statistically, Michael should be holding a minimum-wage job. He should be unable to provide for his children and struggling to hold his head above the poverty line. But he is not. He is a graduate three times over, a provider, an educator, and a meaningful citizen. He is an exceptional exception to the rule. Eighty years, then, is relative.

I've always said that education is liberation. With it, one is capable of gathering what is worth keeping and resisting what requires opposition. Michael understands this adage perhaps better than any man who has been handed his life. When you have to fight for your existence, its importance is compounded and upheld at any cost. When you are not promised tomorrow, immediately its value doubles. According to Michael, life is a cherished race. He runs it this way because he is one of twelve children who had to survive poverty, literacy, and violence. He runs a cherished race in order to guarantee that his children run it the same way. He runs this race to remind God, his mother, and himself that all of his struggles were not wasted. Most importantly, he runs this beautifully cherished race so that he may serve as a beacon of life for the countless children growing up in America and across the world with similar stories.

This very morning, more black men will open their eyes to find prison bars than will wake to venture inside a college classroom. African-American men are more likely to be imprisoned than to earn a college degree. But when you understand and truly believe that you deserve success, you will start to train for something greater. True success comes to those who just won't give up. The difference between those who are ordinary and those who are extraordinary is simply the extra effort added—a denominator in all successful people that proves: success belongs to those who are willing to work for it.

A Promise to Persevere, with its countless examples of the power of faith, is a much needed example of another, more productive, more meaningful way of existing. It will energize your determination with positive thoughts, constructive action and persistent endurance to attain your highest honor. It is a powerful example of how to prepare for ones 80 years of life. And to do so no matter the quantity or quality of our obstacles.

Dr. Ben Carson —
World-Renown Chief Pediatric Neurosurgeon & National Best Selling Author of *Gifted Hands* and *Think Big.*

Introduction

The Race of Life:

Diminished, But Not Finished!

"The race is not given to the fast, nor the swift, nor
the strong, but to he that endured until the end."
                                                -Ecclesiastes 9:11

The scene was Mexico City in 1968. The excitement,
which exuded from the watching masses of people
was pulsating. If you reached for it, you could hold it. Certainly,
you could feel it. A warm, balmy evening, one of many dedicated
to the Centennial Olympic Games, was encouraging this vitality.

In honor of the legendary event, Mexico City didn't sleep.
Children roamed the streets with groups of friends, imitating
their favorite athletes and dreaming of what they might one day
achieve. Elders gathered on their porches and storefronts to
argue about the day's records and of Olympics past. The
spectators who had cheered wildly earlier in the day now reveled
in the aftermath. And the media, represented by nearly every
country on the globe, worked tirelessly to capture the exhilaration.

Earlier, the Ethiopian runner, Mamo Wolde, was first to

cross the finish line in the twenty-six-mile marathon. As he jogged across the finish line, he appeared as fresh as he had when the race started. Behind him, the remaining contenders staggered toward the goal. Some were weary but unhurt; others required medical attention and were rushed to the first-aid stations.

As the day drew to a close, the stadium lights dimmed, the spectators began to leave, and the media crews wrapped up their final segments and sound bites. All that remained was the world-famous Olympic torch — blazing in all its glory.

Suddenly, to the astonishment of the remaining spectators, a lone man stumbled into the stadium. With his right leg broken, bloodied, and bandaged, he hobbled around the four-hundred-meter circuit, wincing with every step. Blood dripped steadily from his elbow. But rather than quit, he tottered relentlessly toward the undulating light of the Olympic torch.

Captivated by this sight — the spectators rose to their feet. With what seemed to be the power of a million hands — they began to applaud him. As he dug deeper into himself and gathered the determination to continue — they applauded. As he summoned the courage to see himself through to the finish line — they applauded. As he continued to stagger and stumble forward with all the energy he had left — they, as a collective crowd, applauded. John Stephen Akhwari, an African runner from Tanzania, had finished last among the seventy-four competitors.

A reporter, sensing an angle for a sarcastic news segment, chased the exhausted and dehydrated Akhwari. Rather than offering the distressed runner a bottle of water or guiding him to a first-aid station, the unsympathetic reporter thrust a microphone into Akhwari's face.

"Don't you know the race is over?" he asked. "Why, after all this time, would you continue running a race that you couldn't win? Why didn't you just quit?"

The exhausted and visibly pained Akhwari looked straight into the camera and declared forthrightly, "I'm a runner from Tanzania! I didn't come seven-thousand miles to *start* the race. I came seven-thousand miles to *finish* the race!" With that, he limped off the track, oblivious to the thundering applause.

Crossing the finish line a full three hours after the conclusion of the arduous race, the injured Akhwari knew that he didn't have to win; he didn't even have to place. But he had to finish, and that goal had kept him going when every logic in the world simply said, "Quit."

Akhwari possessed a rare quality that demonstrated that in the long run, the destination is far more critical than the paths leading to it. No one would have faulted him for dropping out, given the extent of his injuries. Yet, despite the needlessness, he persevered and finished the race.

Go the Distance!

Before you decide to "Go the distance!" you have to ask yourself some very important questions: "What am I running for? What keeps me going in the race of life? Will I give up and stop running my race when I *feel* weary and worn-out?" Chances are, if you're only running life's race simply to run it, you'll be tempted to quit during those painful stretches.

Life is a race. Sometimes it's a series of races (one goal

after another) — some won, some lost, some never completed. Many of us never finish our race because we get sidetracked. For one reason or another, people die with unfulfilled dreams, with unrealized potential, without ever becoming what God intended them to be. As always, the prize goes to those who persevere, to those who hang in there to the finish line, and to those who finish strong.

Anyone who has ever completed the grueling 26.2 miles of a marathon will tell you that every inch of those miles is useless if the runner doesn't cross the finish line. Likewise, if while running the race of life you don't see your goals through to completion, you have gained nothing.

Imagine yourself as an athlete. You're in a coliseum just like the one in Mexico City: A field is at the building's center, and seats surround it. The setting is grand, with thousands of spectators to witness the athletic events that will play out on the stage below them.

Life's race is run in a similar setting — a coliseum of sorts. Every seat in this virtual coliseum is filled. Friends, family members, and neutral spectators are seated in the invisible grandstand, watching your race — waiting to see if you will have a strong finish. Past marathon runners who have overcome tremendous obstacles also occupy seats. Though the people in your coliseum's seats may be invisible to the naked eye, they are quite clear to the spiritual gaze.

Can I Get a Witness?

Hebrews 12:1 proclaims: *"In order to finish the race,*

remember a great cloud of witnesses surround you." Those who surround us are witnesses, not just spectators. The difference between the two is profound. Spectators merely watch you go through something. Witnesses have been through personal trials and tribulations of their own, hardships that mimic yours. Their view of you is supportive; it is compassionate and understanding. These witnesses, despite their difficult ordeals, have found ways to finish their races, and their successes should encourage your victory.

There is nothing like hearing the testimony of someone who has survived a battle similar to your own to bolster your faith and courage. You are better equipped to finish your own race when someone proves that it can and has been done. Testimonies empower you to believe that you can finish the race. They encourage you to hold on — and to believe that you will overcome your obstacles. You must always remember the witnesses surrounding you and call on their testimonies to fuel your race.

When I look at the seats around the coliseum where I'm running my current race, I see many witnesses rooting for me: Harriet Tubman and Frederick Douglass, Sojourner Truth and Malcolm X, Martin Luther King Jr. and Fannie Lou Hamer, Marcus Garvey and Mary McLeod Bethune, W.E.B. Dubois and Paul Lawrence Dunbar, Booker T. Washington and Carter G. Woodson, A. Philip Randolph and Paul Robeson, Benjamin Elijah Mays and Benjamin Banneker, King Shaka Zulu and King Hannibal. Certainly, you have your own list of witnesses who are rooting for you. If you hush the noise of humanity, you may actually hear them. To have your past ancestors cheering for you is to have triumph guaranteed. Remember, "He who has run the race before us, runs it now with us."

Like John Stephen Akhwari in the Mexico City Olympics, I made a promise to persevere. I had many false starts, stumbles, and falls, but now, in the prime of my life, I'm progressing. I'm succeeding, not as a man for whom the best is over, but as a runner who is dashing toward the finish line with my eyes on the glorious prize.

Part 1
"We Fall Down..."

"Our greatest glory is not in falling, but in rising every time we fall."
                                        -Confucius

How Did I Get Here?

I almost died at twenty-five. I swallowed two hundred pills, one after the other, with Heaven on my mind. Whether or not God would have me after taking my own life was to be seen, but even the possibility of Him denying my salvation could not dissuade me. It was 1998 and I wasn't many things—I wasn't a father to my children, I wasn't a high school graduate or literate, I wasn't employed, I wasn't mentally stable, I wasn't a son...or at least it felt that way with Dennie Miller Sr. buried beneath a plot of earth at Arbutus Memorial Park. He had died before I could fully love him, before I could know the true depth and width of his love. I don't know that even he could have saved me, though.

I had paged my buddy, Jay, to tell him I was in trouble. I spelled "9-1-1" with a trembling finger, so he'd hurry and call me back. When he called, I was going to tell him I had a beef and needed to hold his gun. When he brought it to me, I would say "thank you" and something sincere, something to let him know not to take my death personally, and then I would hold the gun against my temple, feel its chilliness and then its dull bullet, and then everything would be all right. Only Jay never called back, and my dying could not be put off any longer, so I stuffed my mouth with Tylenol and ate dozens and dozens of capsules as if they were candy.

In the hospital, a nurse warned me, "Don't you fall asleep. Don't you fall asleep, Michael, unless you want not to ever wake up again." And the gravity of what I had done weighed down on me.

"Please God, please," I said. "Let me get up from here, God. Let me get up from here and I promise to make everything right. I *'promise to persevere'* and run life's race like I mean it!"

Chapter 1

A False Start:
My Humble Beginnings

"Success is to be measured not so much by the position that one has reached in life as by the obstacles which one has to overcome while trying to succeed."
—Booker T. Washington

false start - *noun.* an unsuccessful attempt to begin something.

A stadium hushes. Hundreds of spectators inhale and hold their collective breath. Below them, a single row of 100-meter finalists prepares for a race that will last about ten seconds. The runners press their fingertips into the track, placing their hands on the starting line like pool players lining up a break.

Pointing the gun toward Heaven, the starter judge yells, *"Set!"* In one quick, catlike motion, the runners brace their backs and crouch against their starting blocks. Each sprinter is poised for victory. Each has trained daily, working to near exhaustion. Each is the sharpest, the swiftest, and the strongest

15

of his kind. For each, this race is crucial.

But have they trained their minds?

The runner who breaks the tape will need more than physical prowess, more than a sturdy heart, and more than strong lungs. He will also need concentration, control, and confidence. Ultimately, he must possess an unerring eye for the finish line. At this tense moment, one mis-timed twitch or slight bend of the knee could trigger a false start and cost him the race. But if he hesitates, if he shifts on the starting block even slightly, his initial steps will lag behind his competitors, guaranteeing a loss.

"Bang!...*Bang!*"

The second shot fired signals that a runner has made a false start.

Many of us set goals that will enhance the quality of our lives, but for one reason or another, we fail to reach the finish line. The gun goes off and we're off...

Bang!...*Bang!*

Sometimes we start too soon. Our inner voice whispers: *"Wait!, not now."* But in our enthusiasm, we only hear, *"Go!"* We are so anxious that we jump on an idea before the time is right. With our rhythm thrown off, our game plan is shot, resulting in embarrassment, discouragement, and loss of momentum. We missed our opportunity. We have to start over.

Bang!...*Bang!*

Or we start too late. This time the inner voice says, *"Go!"* But we hesitate, and only hear, *"Wait, not now."* Sometimes the signal to start comes as a surprise. Maybe we were hoping for

16

this, but when it comes, we're thrown into a state of shock. We freeze, and this momentary paralysis is enough to cost us a victory in the race we've always dreamed of winning.

Bang!...

Then there are those who give up along the way. If you repeatedly failed to lose weight, quit smoking, return to your studies, or spend more time with your family, the race eventually begins to feel pointless. Once you feel beaten, you become unwilling or unable to finish it.

But that's all right. If you want to get back into the race, you must go back to where it all started, the "starting blocks"— where your first series of "false starts" occurred. You must recognize that you are where you are supposed to be, and that you've done what was necessary to reach this point. Know that the lane assigned to you is *still* yours to claim for victory. Focus on the starter's gun, hoping not to make another false start. Remain in your own lane. Kneel down, press your fingertips into the track, brace your back and crouch against your starting block, and *begin again!*

My Journey

The first of my many false starts grew out of my humble beginnings. I was born and raised in a West Baltimore ghetto called Sandtown. My family, the poorest in the community, lived less than four blocks from where the heartbreaking HBO miniseries, The *Corner* was filmed and took place.

In my neighborhood, being book-smart meant you were a nerd, and therefore, an outcast. But going to jail and surviving your sentence made you a hero. Some local criminals went to jail, but many got away with their heinous crimes. The ones who didn't get arrested roamed the streets at night–dealing drugs, commiting gang violence, and murders. Somehow, they seemed to elude the local police officers. The crimes, I presume, were far too many for the cops to keep up with.

Most of the people in my neighborhood seemed to glorify the "ghetto fabulous" lifestyle. But being "ghetto fabulous" is an oxymoron, because there's no way you can be both "ghetto" and "fabulous."

For instance, in Sandtown, there were fragments of broken glass scattered all over the streets, but we called that "fabulous." The elementary schools were substandard and employed inexperienced teachers who were forced to use six-year-old textbooks, yet we called that "fabulous." The neighborhood stores charged us double for milk, meat, produce, and gasoline, yet we called that "fabulous." The police befriended us but didn't arrest the culprits who were known for selling drugs in our community, and we called that "fabulous." We celebrated being "ghetto fabulous" and considered it a badge of honor, rather than a reflection of our destitution.

A cramped, three-bedroom house I called *home* accommodated many people: my parents and my eleven brothers and sisters. My mother gave birth to five girls and seven boys. I was the baby-boy. My parents slept in the front bedroom, my sisters in the middle bedroom, and all us boys slept in the back bedroom in two twin beds, crammed like sardines in a can.

Our bedroom was so small we had to walk sideways to get

between the two beds. One dresser with two broken drawers held all of our clothes, but since we had so few of them, there was always plenty of drawer space. My mother purchased most of our clothes—and nearly everything else our household required—from the local thrift stores.

Linoleum covered the kitchen and bathroom floors. The rest of the house had worn-out, painted, hardwood floors that squeaked and gave us splinters if we walked across them barefoot. Some of the floors even had missing planks that exposed the dry, rotted wood underneath.

Paint and plaster peeled from the ceilings and walls. The ceiling leaked whenever it rained. For this, my mother placed pots and pans around the house to catch the drips. In winter, cold air whistled through our windows and hugged our bodies tight.

Despite the condition of our house, our daily inspiration came from a steel plaque hanging above the mantel in the living room. It read, "Dear God, Bless This House. It May Be Small, But It's Big Enough For Love And That's All." The plaque stood as a monument of faith and encouragement. God's blessings on our house were far more important than its size, and His Love kept us warm.

Talk-Back-to-You Shoes

My shoes were what we called *talk-back-to-you* shoes. The front or "mouth" part was always torn and flapped open as I walked. I often wore my shoes until the soles had worn through and my feet scraped the ground. As a temporary remedy, I would cut some cardboard from a box and put it inside the shoes

19

to protect my feet. But I didn't complain—I was young and poor, but always willing to do whatever it took to survive.

We're Marching to Zion

Before we went to church, my parents required us to take part in Sunday morning devotions. At 6:30 a.m. we began singing children's songs like, "The B-i-b-l-e, That's The Book For Me." Afterward, my mother would take the leftover change she'd saved over the week and buy us treats.

No matter how we looked while playing outside, my mother made sure we put on our best clothes before going into "Da House of da Lawd." Just as she did before we left for school, she would line us up for inspection and make sure our teeth were brushed, our faces washed, and our clothes ironed. Before we left for church we were always presentable.

Attending church was not an option—it was a requirement. We belonged to Zion Hill Missionary Baptist Church where my father held several church offices—treasurer, deacon, member of the board of trustees—and he sung in the church's male chorus. Zion Hill was so small that when our pastor asked, "Would the choir please stand?" almost the entire congregation rose. In fact, about half of that congregation was my family.

We would march in there like an army, taking up two of the church's four small benches. Whenever we misbehaved in church, my mother would remind us, "This here is da House of da Lawd. Don't y'all be playin' in God's House now, ya hear?" She would always catch us, discipline us, and then go right back to praising the Lord—all within the same breath.

20

Once, my mom was singing a Gospel song and clapping the tambourine as my brothers and I were playing around. While still on beat, she leaned over, wrung my ears like two wash rags, slapped one of my brothers with her tambourine, and then went right back to praising the Lord...as if nothing ever happened.

My mother was a gentle, soft-spoken, bashful Christian woman who was generally quiet—until you rubbed her the wrong way. When that happened, she didn't hesitate to speak her mind. She'd tell her children, relatives, or even our school-teachers exactly what she was feeling and what she thought they should do about it.

It was my mother who managed the finances with my father's limited income. She was able to stretch my father's paycheck to pay the rent and utility bills, buy clothes when needed, and still have money leftover for groceries. One of her frequently repeated adages was, "The Lawd will make a way out of no way...somehow!

As a wife and mother, caring for a household and raising a large family under arduous circumstances, my mother had to endure all sorts of struggles. Many people unfairly ridiculed her, making her feel like an outcast. Neighbors and friends felt my mother had made terrible decision after terrible decision by giving birth to so many children. They would say things like, "Why would she have so many children? Doesn't she know how poor she is? How can she provide for all of those children? Why doesn't she have a job?" They often chastised my mother even within her presence. No one ever seemed to acknowledge that my father was equally as responsible. These self-proclaimed critics did not try to conceal their disapproval of my family's size, either. But in the midst of all the naysayers, my mother trusted that God would provide, and continued to care for her twelve children as best she could.

My Aunt and Uncle would occasionally volunteer to help raise some of us. They always suggested that they rear the youngest ones—Sandra, Jeffrey, and me—but, my mom wouldn't entertain any such idea. She intended to keep her family together and to ensure that we were raised with the same morals, values, and principles to which *she* prescribed.

It wasn't so much *what* people said about my mom that disappointed her. Rather, it was *who*. Some of my mom's closest friends and family members, the same people she looked to for moral support, would congregate and criticize her. It was only her determined faith that God would be a friend to the friendless that sustained her during those difficult moments.

Regardless of the cynics, she continued to fulfill her duties as a mother, countering the criticism with scriptural references like, *"Through Christ, all things are possible."* When situations seemed unbearable, she reminded us, *"God will never put more on you than you can bear."* When the burdens seemed too heavy for her to carry, she declared, *"He's my burden-bearer, my heavy-load carrier!"* When we were confused about what to do, where to go, or how to get whatever we wanted or needed, she proclaimed, *"Ask and it shall be given. Seek and you shall find. Knock and the door shall be opened."* Her faith enabled her to endure the strife.

No matter what happened to my mother or how hard she struggled to raise her family on my father's meager income, she viewed each new day as a blessing. She often said, "The true blessing in life is not a new car, a new house, or having lots of money. It is just being able to see a new day. So, every day is a good day! He woke me up this morning and started me on my way! And for that, I'm thankful!"

She would reminisce about how good God is and go into one of her metaphysical states where she would lift up her hands and cry out, *"Thank ya, Jesus! Thank ya!"*

Whenever my father wanted to call my name, he would start with my oldest brother's name and go through each of my other brothers' names in descending order until finally he spoke, "Michael!"

"Ah, Ronnie. I mean, ah...Kelly. Ah...Dennie...I mean, ah...Donnell. No, Jeffrey. Um...Michael. Yeah, Michael. Come downstairs and take out dis here crash [trash] and put 'tin back-yard, ah, ri-ri-ri-right now."

My father, who often stuttered, had only an eighth-grade education. A native Southerner, full of resilience and determination, he had dropped out of school to provide for his parents by working on a farm.

That same motivation was exemplified in my father's care for his wife and children. My father desired the very best for his family. He could foresee a better way of life for us, always reminding us that the conditions could "get better than this." He worked from six in the morning until six in the evening for a construction company. My father drove the company's red bus, which my family affectionately called "Big Red." One of his primary responsibilities was picking up his coworkers in the morning, taking them to work, and then driving them back home at the end of the workday. Dropping everyone off meant that he would occasionally arrive home very late.

Desperately craving for some of my father's attention, I often watched and waited for Big Red to come down the street. As soon as I spotted the crimson bus coming over the hump of Fulton Street, I would race down the block and follow Big Red to the bottom of Riggs Avenue, and then into the lot where my father usually parked it.

"Daddy, Daddy, how was work today?" I'd ask.

In a tired, dragged-out voice, my dad would respond, "All right."

Never Walk with Your Back Bent

One particular evening, when I was about nine years old, I raced down Riggs Avenue to greet my father, as usual. He responded in his typically unaffectionate manner, but I didn't care. I yearned for his attention.

Walking in a slow, tired slouch with his back bent, my dad dragged his feet toward our house, which stood in the middle of the block. Willing to do anything to get his attention, I started imitating his walk. Eventually, he looked over and saw me mimicking him. He said in a loud, thunderous voice, "Boy, don'chu evah do dat again. Nevah walk with yo' back bent like dat again. You unda'stand?"

"Yes, sir," I answered, with tears in my eyes.

"Boy, don'chu evah, and I mean *evah*, do dat again. Ya hear me, son?"

"Yes, sir," I said again. "But, Daddy," I protested, my voice cracking, "I was just trying to get your attention. I just want to be like you, Daddy."

"Boy, I don't give a damn and don't care, ah, wha-wha-wha-, what-chu say! Ain't no excuse fa-fa-fa-for it! Nevah walk with your back bent over like dat again! I mean it!"

With my back now straightened, I wiped the tears from my eyes. My dad always said boys weren't supposed to cry.

"Daddy," I asked him, "why can't I walk like you, with my back bent over, too? I was just trying to be like you."

He looked at me with his tired, bloodshot-red eyes and said, "Because, son, when you walk with ya' back bent over, people can ride ya' back. You see, I *have* to walk like this. I can't cry [try] to walk up straight to save my life. But, Michael, ya' still young, and ya' got a chance to walk wit' your head up high, with a straight back...with pride!"

I will never forget that moment. Normally my dad stuttered, but on that sunny evening, his words resonated like thunder, and I stood staring at him, stunned by his wisdom. Ever since that day, I have tried to walk with my back straight. The philosophy behind his statement was quite clear. Simply put: "People can't ride your back unless you bend it."

After my dad got off work, he took a shower, ate dinner, and then went to his second job. We couldn't make ends meet without this extra stream of income. At that second job, he put his life on the line as a hack, operating as a gypsy taxi in

Sandtown. Often, he worked all night for just a few dollars, only to lose those dollars later when robbed at gunpoint. As depicted in *The Corner*, Sandtown was poverty-stricken and rampant with gangs, drugs, and violence.

Ideally, the weekend is an opportune time for a son to spend time with his father. But for me, weekends were anything but father-son time. In addition to everything else he did, my father sang with a traveling gospel quartet on weekends. His quartet was not a big-time group, and they weren't paid for their services. Rather, their performances were considered a ministry, part of their evangelical service to God. Because the group traveled to sing, my dad stayed busy on the weekends and spent a lot of time away from the family.

Technically, I grew up with my father in my house, but because of his many other obligations, he was rarely home. Thus, I was almost as deprived as any fatherless child. My father's work duties made me feel like his spending time with me didn't matter. Of course, I failed to recognize that he was out providing for the household. Never mind that he had to sacrifice nearly all of his time to provide food, clothing, and shelter for us. Never mind that without him, my family wouldn't have been able to survive. Never mind that he was called by God to use his voice to spread the Gospel to others. Regardless of his sacrifices, I still wanted his attention as soon as he walked through the door. I didn't talk about this with my parents or my older brothers and sisters, though, because my family's attitude was that I, as a child, didn't have a voice, much less an opinion. I would have preferred an open relationship in which I could have respectfully expressed how I felt, but in my family, children were supposed to be *seen* and not *heard*.

. Besides providing for his wife and children, he was incredibly dedicated to his parents, and trekked down to North Carolina whenever they needed him. At times, my father would go to North Carolina every weekend for a month straight. He supported his parents physically, emotionally, spiritually, and financially. His dedication to them taught me a lot about truly honoring my own parents.

If You Can't Find a Way, Make One!

Both of my parents stressed the importance of finding every possible way to survive. Although there were many obstacles to overcome, my mother never worried about how we were going to make it or how difficult it might be to survive. She just did what she had to do. As I mentioned earlier, my mother managed our meager finances. My father also found ways to make it. For example, he would drain gas from the company truck with a water hose. Once the gas started to come out, he would hold the hose over a bucket, and then put the gas in our car. You may call it stealing, but we called it surviving.

Although the people around us were poor, it seemed to me that they had all the finer things in life. Mrs. Naomi and her two sons, Ricky and Robby, lived in the corner house on our block. She often gave her sons money to buy their dinner from the corner carryout. They would bring home a sub-shop bag that included the usual: a cheese steak or a cheeseburger sub, French fries, and a bottle of soda. You could smell the subs, even if you were locked in the house, and lying under three blankets. I used to get upset and think, *Dang, I gotta go in here and eat these leftover neck bones, black-eyed peas, and collard greens, while they eat subs and French fries everyday. Man, are they lucky!*

My father, however, had resolved not to surrender to welfare, and this promise meant his income was our sole support. Divided among so many children, his money diminished quickly, but his pride did not. No matter our troubles, his work supported us and *that* he could live with. And while he labored, my mother held the house together. She was its contour, its glue, its foundation. When the government cheese and canned meat were passed out, we watched our neighbors collect their monthly aid from behind our thrift store curtains. We understood poverty well and knew that the aid kept many of our neighbors alive, and that the food would've been very much welcomed in our own house. But my father condemned charity and believed an honest struggle was worth a world more than a single handout. He taught us not to judge, but also not to surrender.

Sure, there were times we ate well, and there were many occasions when we were forced to make do with what we had. Bread fried with lard in a cast-iron skillet made "wish" sandwiches. You know, the kind where you wished you had some meat. We were grateful for the times we'd gotten our hands on a big block of welfare cheese (unbeknownst to my father) because we'd take that cheese, slice it and dice it to utter perfection, slap it in the cast-iron frying pan, and make the best grilled-cheese sandwiches ever! We often fried bologna, watched it make a big bubble of itself in the cast iron pan and made a feast of that, too. I, myself, was a master ghetto chef. My specialty was ghetto yat gaw mein. I would take a delicious mix of oodles of noodles, boil some eggs, add ketchup, a pinch of Season-All, and voila! That was my idea of yat gaw mein.

Birthdays Were the Worst Days!

Poverty permeates everything and is evident even in the details. My family and I never celebrated birthdays with parties. In fact, the only birthday party I can remember ever going to was for my buddy, Jay. Like everyone else in Sandtown, Jay's family was poor and birthdays were generally no cause for excitement. But Jay's mom must have thought her son's tenth year shouldn't pass without some sort of recognition because she attempted to give him a party.

Six of us attended, and our entertainment consisted of running around the backyard and all over the house for a couple of hours. When the time came to sing "Happy Birthday," Jay's mother tiptoed from the kitchen, balancing a Chocolate Junior Tasty Cake not bigger than a fist in her palm. A candle shaped like the number ten was pushed into its frosting and took up as much space as the cake itself. We sang to Jay and then watched his mom cut the Chocolate Junior into six identical parts. We opened our mouths a single time, chewed maybe three-quarters of a chew, and swallowed the bite-sized pieces. It never dawned on us that a Chocolate Junior Tasty Cake wasn't a classic birthday cake, that we might have gotten a bowl full of ice cream in another world, or that we were unbearably poor. We just ate the big crumbs and kept it moving.

Making a Way Out of No Way

There were times when it seemed we had absolutely nothing to eat. In those stomach-growling moments, my mother made a way out of what seemed to be no way at all. She was a connoisseur of those make-a-way-out-of-no-way meals. She would reach into the seemingly empty kitchen cabinet, get those welfare-canned meats with the "Not-For-Sale" label on them, and create a piping hot concoction that filled our bellies for the night. I don't know what type of meat it was, or what else she would put into her pot. But whatever it was, it was delicious!

I always danced when it was time to eat (I still do even today).

"Michael, Michael, Michael!" my mother would shout.

I'd answer, "Huh?"

"Boy, don't you 'huh' me. Sit down like you've got some sense, before I knock you in the middle of next week!"

Quickly, I'd reply, "Yes ma'am."

No matter the circumstance, the golden rule was that no one ate until the man of the house arrived home from work. This rule was supreme. We'd sit with aching bellies until my father came through the door, bent over from a hard day's work. Only after he had blessed the food could we eat, and always, we did so as a family. During the prayer, he always took a parenthetical pause and transitioned from blessing the food to praying for us. He would be gracious and proclaim, "Lawd, we

30

may not have much, but we are gonna thank you anyhow. Thank ya, Heavenly Father, for the food that will nourish our bodies. Thank ya for my wife, for it was her hands that prepared it. And oh Father God, bless my chil'ren one by one! Even when dey go astray, Lawd, wheel 'em back into de ark of safety. Help 'em, Lawd, to understand, dat in times of trouble ta jus' lean on you." It was something special about when my father prayed. I always felt secure. To know that he trusted tomorrow would be brighter gave me a strong sense of safety...and hope.

We did have a bit of money for treats, though. When our father came home, he would give each of us a nickel, a dime, or even a quarter to buy some candy. One day, my siblings and I complained to our father that we were hungry. He gave us fifteen cents each and told us to go the corner bar to buy a bag of Mrs. Ihries potato chips. We'd put ketchup in the bag, shake it, and had a meal. No, we didn't have much. But through it all, we learned to make a way when there seemed to be no way at all.

It Pays to Be Persistent

As you run the race of life, you will find that it *pays* to be *persistent*. Many years ago, a large American shoe manufacturer sent two sales reps out to different parts of the Australian Outback. They wanted to determine if they could drum up some business among the Aborigines. Some time later, the company received telegrams from both agents. The first one said, "No business here. The natives don't wear shoes." The second one said, "Great opportunity here. The natives don't wear shoes!" Just as the second salesman, we have to learn how to turn lemons into lemonade, and how to view obstacles as opportunities, trusting that every setback is a setup for a blessing in our lives.

I've always been a hustler. I learned at an early age that I would have to work hard for any material possessions. From the time I was five years old, I searched for and worked menial jobs on the streets of West Baltimore. I would walk about a mile from my house to Lafayette Market or even as far as two miles to Lexington Market just to run errands. Each time, I made sure to come home with something in my pocket.

I even carried bags at the grocery store. I'd ask some unsuspecting or not-so unsuspecting woman, "Excuse me, ma'am, may I carry yo' bags?"

"No, thanks. Thanks, anyway," she would say. "And what are you doing here, anyway? You're just a baby."

I would persist. "Oh, I can carry them, ma'am. I'm seven years old now." Actually, I was only five, but determined and persistent.

"But the bags are bigger than you."

Assuring her that she didn't have to pay me, that I would carry them for free, I would grab the bags without waiting for a response.

"Well, since you insist..." and I'd follow her to her car. On most occasions, the customer would end up giving me a fifty-cent food-stamp coin, a quarter, or some spare change. I didn't care. I was a little hustler.

At other times, I pumped gas and begged for change at a local Amoco station, "Excuse me, ma'am (or sir), can I please pump your gas?"

"No, that's okay," they'd reply.

And just as I did when I was carrying grocery bags at the food market, I would say assertively, "No problem. I'll do it free," hoping that the customer would have mercy on a poor child and give me some spare change. Most of the time, it worked.

Being in a poor community meant that poor people surrounded me. Just as they did at the food market, the gas station customers would give me a few pennies and nickels. If I was really lucky, I got a wrinkled one-dollar food stamp. "Thank you, ma'am, thank you so much," I would respond. I was grateful, but I was also determined. Every time I went to the gas station, I maintained the faith that I would walk away with something. Even a penny was better than what I had—nothing.

At the gas station I learned persistence. I never let a customer tell me "no." Even if the customers didn't want me to pump their gas, I was confident that my charisma would triumph. When they said, "Young man, I'm telling you that I don't have any money to pay you," I would reply, "Listen, you don't have to worry 'bout anythang, sir. I'll take care of everythang." Usually, my charm would pay off and I would walk away with some spare change.

No matter what the weather or season, I found a way to earn money. If I wasn't pumping gas or carrying grocery bags, I was scrubbing the neighbor's marble steps in the spring, cutting grass in the summer, raking leaves in the fall, or shoveling snow in the winter. If I couldn't find a way, I *made* a way.

Be Persistent, Not a Pest

Now, it pays to be *persistent*, but not a *pest*. Occasionally, persistence can get you in trouble. One time, a customer at the gas station kept telling me "no," but I refused to take "no" for an answer.

I said, "Sir, I'll pump the gas. I'll take care of everythang for free."

He said, "Young man, don't you touch my car or dare put gas in it. This is a brand-new Cadillac, and I don't want anybody touching it." I looked at his beautiful, black Cadillac and said to myself, *"I know he got some money!"*

As soon as he went inside the Amoco to pay for his gas, I heard him boast to the clerk, "Give me a fill up on number two, please." While he was flirting with the woman behind the counter, asking her if she wanted to go for a ride in his new Caddy, I grabbed the hose to pump his gas. Right then I caught a glimpse of a kid riding the very bike I'd always wanted but couldn't afford—a Mongoose. I was drawn to the machine's beauty—how its metal glistened in the sun. The mag wheels rolled round and round and put me in a daze. I stared at that bike for a good two minutes, imagining myself on it, pedaling fast as the devil, and my shirt rippling in the wind. I was totally unfocused on the gas I didn't have permission to pump in the first place. When I finally gained my composure, and returned to the task at hand, I realized that instead of filling up the tank, I was filling up the Cadillac's back seat. Gasoline was everywhere. The owner ran toward me shouting, "Hey, what the hell are you doing?" I didn't answer. My heart was beating so fast that I thought it would leap out of my chest. I just hauled tail, running and dodging through the streets and alleys, praying I wouldn't get caught. And while I didn't, I learned a valuable lesson: You can push the limits of persistence.

But There's Still Hope!

Persistence leads to success most of the time. Most successful people have had more failures than successes, but the more often they stumble and fall, the more often they pick themselves up and get going again. This is because persistence is directly linked to desire. If you want something bad enough, you will develop the mind-set and energy level to overcome all the obstacles between you and that goal.

The biggest difference between people who succeed and people who don't is not usually talent, but persistence. Many brilliant people give up. Harriet Tubman, one of the most persistent leaders in history, never abandoned her formidable mission to bring slaves safely through the Underground Railroad. She gave her passengers two choices: Either escape to the North for freedom or suffer death by her rifle. People who are highly successful don't quit, regardless of their false starts. Successful people are ordinary people who have fallen down, but have gotten back up again.

In any given race, if the start is not fair, the starter must declare a false start. In some athletic events, a false start can immediately disqualify an athlete from further competition. Usually the referee will give one warning. This official typically determines whether a start is a success.

If some self-appointed official has convinced you that one false start dooms you to permanent failure, then that "official" is wrong. From a spiritual perspective, your destination in life is not determined by a referee's judgment of your actions. Man does not have the last word. In God's eyes, there is no limit to the number of false starts you can have—you are allowed an infinite number. God always allows us to start over again, regardless of our false starts.

No matter how many false starts you've had in the past, you must go back to the starting line and begin again. But this time I caution you to consider: Who told you that you were disqualified from the race? Who told you that you were worth nothing? Who told you that just because you failed once, you'll never amount to anything? Who defied God's divine order, which declares, All things are possible for those who believe?

Above all, you must stay in the race. It takes sheer persistence and an unwavering determination to reach the finish line. Growing up, I was grateful for having the type of parents who demonstrated the willpower that is needed to finish a race. I remember once asking my mom, who was cooking in the kitchen at the time, "Mama, what would you do if you were suddenly told that you were going to die tonight?" She replied, "I'm gonna finish cooking these neck bones and black-eye peas so dat when yo' daddy come home, he'll have somethin' to eat."...Now that's determination!

Chapter 2

Lay Aside Every Weight:

Are You a Heavyweight Champion?

"Let us lay aside every weight and the wrongdoings
that cling so closely."

—Hebrews 12:1

weight - *verb*. the state of being ponderous,
burdened, impeded, oppressed, or handicapped.

It is important to know how to get over your false starts,
but it's equally as important to know how to run your
race. If we want to finish the race, we must remove the excess
baggage we carry. I have never seen track stars run with heavy
coats on their backs and weights in their shoes. It doesn't take a
Ph.D. in aero-dynamics to understand that running with
baggage will slow you down. Dr. Brad R. Braxton writes:

> We harbor attitudes and engage in behaviors that wrap
> around our feet, causing us to stumble rather than to
> sprint. The writer of Hebrews, Chapter 12 exhorts us to
> remove these hindrances.

From Discovery to Recovery

Many of us are not able to persevere because we are still carrying the baggage from our past to avoid one gift we should accept—pain. Pain is a gift nobody wants. But if it weren't for pain, how would we know what to change? A life run by emotions (or how we "feel") is like a roller coaster ride—up and down, round and round.

As children, we were put on the ride without our permission and as adults we don't know how to get off, so we just hold on and holler. We must *uncover* to *discover* before we can *recover* from the *pain* of our *past*. There is a saying that goes, "time heals all wounds," but that's not necessarily so. There are wounds that worsen with time. There are wounds that can only be healed through exposure to the light of truth. The problem is that no one is talking about their personal struggles, so we learn to "suffer in silence."

We're always trying to dress up the body, instead of building up the mind. You see, it's easier to dress up than to grow up. We try to cover up by achieving material success, but that only works when we're with others. The void and emptiness returns when we're alone with ourselves. In a way, we're like dressed-up garbage cans–so full of crap it stinks up the other areas of our lives. Then our children become trash collectors, collecting all of our mental and emotional garbage, and the cycle continues.

But if you choose to ignore yesterday, if you choose not to acknowledge your past demons and disregard your personal history, your present life will be stationary and your future life certainly not much more. I had to go back and deal with every-thing from my childhood and adolescence that I'd swept under the carpet. I was going through life battling my past problems subconsciously because I was afraid to deal with them con-sciously. I was suppressing the pain, thinking that if I censored it I'd stop hurting. I didn't know it would come back to haunt and hurt me later. To fix my present life, I had to go back to where it all started—my childhood. It's important to appreciate the difference between your childhood and the memory of your childhood. Your childhood is not what causes you pain; it's the memory of your childhood that pains you. And that memory, which brings energy, can drain you for the rest of your life if you do not confront it. I had to face those inner demons.

Dealing with Death

Though I was a swift runner who seemed to elude people and circumstances in my life, there were things I couldn't escape, things I couldn't outrun. I've carried a lot of baggage in my life. The death of my two sisters was quite possibly the heaviest of all.

Even now, it's emotionally taxing for me to write about witnessing the traumatic deaths of my two sisters. I was just three years old at the time. My mother was now left with eleven children—my brother Tyrone had died at age one from SIDS (Sudden Infant Death Syndrome) before I was born.

All of my other brothers and sisters were in school that day, except my older sister, Shelia and my younger sister, Neicy.

Neicy and I were waiting impatiently for something to eat so, my mother asked Sheila, who was helping her around the house, to make my favorite meal—hotdogs with pork and beans. I walked into the kitchen with Sheila and my little sister, Neicy, who was about two years old. My mother went upstairs to take a nap.

Sheila sat Neicy in her high chair and began boiling the hotdogs and warming up the pork and beans. Neicy was crying because she was hungry, and I was acting out because I couldn't wait any longer to eat. Sheila was going back and forth between the table and the stove, setting up the plate for me, attending to Neicy, and cooking the food.

Sheila chopped some of the hot dogs into bite-size pieces and placed them on the table. As Sheila was walking back to the stove to get the pork and beans, Neicy grabbed and stuffed a whole hot dog into her mouth and began to choke on it. I stood there watching, helplessly, not knowing what to do. It wasn't until Sheila came back to the table that she realized Neicy was choking. She grabbed Neicy and laid her across her lap, repeatedly thrusting her hands into Neicy's mouth, doing everything she could to free the hotdog from her throat.

Neicy continued to strain and fight for air, while Sheila tried desperately to keep her from choking. The more I saw Neicy struggle, the more I cried. To her demise, and our dismay, Neicy choked to death within a matter of minutes. I vividly remember watching, without understanding, what was happening. All I knew was that I never saw my little sister, my playmate, and my best friend ever again.

Family members rushed to console us. Many of them were

especially worried about my mother. After absorbing the loss of a second child, she tried to remain calm and copastetic around everyone. Concerned friends and family members would sympathetically ask, "Nellie, are you all right?" and she would respond, "Child, I'm fine. The Lawd will make a way... somehow." But behind closed doors while my brothers and sisters were in school and family and friends weren't around, I would watch her weep. As she worked around the house, she mourned, and because I was the baby, I was the sole witness to her pain.

As my mother cried secretly over the next few months, I, too, began to grieve deeply for the loss of my sister and playmate, Neicy. Despite my young age and my failure to fully understand where Neicy had gone, I felt guilty. I carried that guilt well into adulthood, really until the completion of this book. I had just stood there and done nothing. Prior to Neicy's death, I always pretended I was a superhero who could save the world. There was nothing I could not defeat. If it appeared that someone or something was dead, I used my magic wand and superhero powers to save them, just as heroes in the cartoons did.

One particular morning, when my mother was feeling real low, I garnered my imaginary wand–a tree branch—from the backyard. I was going to bring my sister back to life.

"Don't worry mama. Don't cry. I'll bring Neicy back to life. You'll see. All I have to do is keep using my magical powers and she'll be here before you know it."

After my arm had fatigued from making hundreds of hopeful circles with the wand and my jaw had stiffened from repeating, "Neicy, come back," I finally realized my super hero powers were useless. I couldn't use my magical beam to rescue my sister. After that, I stopped imagining I had superpowers and could save the world. I stopped imagining at all.

I wish I'd have never stopped daydreaming; my dreams took me beyond my reality and it's always good to imagine things beyond what you can see with the natural eye. Because I was looking at the material rather than the spiritual world, I never imagined Neicy was with God. She always remained at the kitchen table where I left her, with me standing there, not knowing what to do. Therefore, I carried this secret trauma for years to come. Just as a young Ray Charles stood there in the movie Ray, not knowing what to do when his brother died, I, too, had stood idly by.

No, Not Again

Six months after the devastation of Neicy's death, I lost another sister—Jacqualina. I was three-and-a-half years old, and Jacqualina was a newborn baby. I was upstairs with my mother, taking a nap in her bed, where I always slept because it felt like home. Although Jacqualina's crib was next to my mother's bed, that day she was sleeping with my sister, Towanda, in Towanda's room. Towanda leaned over Jacqualina to wake her up, and she wouldn't move. I walked into the room to find out why Towanda was screaming. I later learned that Jacqualina had died from the complication of Down Syndrome.

Losing two sisters in one year was too much for me to handle. I couldn't bear to see it happen again. Obviously, the loss was overwhelming for my mother as well, who had given birth to twelve children, only to see nine survive. She tried to maintain her strength for her surviving children, but burying three of her babies was beyond devastating, and eventually the bereavement began its toll.

She cried a lot. Sometimes for hours at a time. And once again, because I was the baby and was home with her while the others were away, I was the lonely witness to her sorrow. She tried with everything she had to maintain a tough image–she was raising six boys and three girls who looked to her for strength–and she succeeded a good majority of the time. But with the sweet substance of the family gone, she collapsed and became a sad pile of weeping and bones.

At Jacqualina's funeral, my mother abandoned the tough image. There, in front of her baby's coffin, she finally released the pent-up emotions. In front of everyone, she screamed from the bottom of her stomach until all she could manage was whispers and petite coughs. She cried and moaned, "Lawd, why? Please don't take my Jaqualina away from me, Lawd! Neicy just left me! I can't take it anymore! Why, Lawd, why?"

That was a very emotional time for her. I guess any parent would feel that way. She had just lost my brother, Tyrone, a few years earlier, and now she had to face losing two daughters in the same year. As time went on, my mother began to move beyond the deaths of her daughters and to accept the reality that they were gone. She used to say, "God knew that I had too many children, so he called my other three children home." She began to understand that, though they were her Earthly children, they were principally Children of God. They were put into her life as a gift from God and taken as he saw fit. As Mama gave her problems to God instead of trying to shoulder them herself, she began to open up to others about her pain, and consequently her healing began. Closer to the end of her somber journey, she would proclaim, "Weeping may endure for a night, but Joy comes in the morning."

Lessons of Grief

From my mother's grieving, I learned two very important lessons. The first was that you never "get over" the death of a loved one. Many of us imagine that we're going crazy when we just can't seem to recover from the loss of someone. But their loss was not meant to be gotten over. The spirit and memory of the departed is meant to be carried with you forever, so that they can be remembered and cherished.

Second, I learned some priceless ways to live with such profound tragedy. Grief is an ongoing process that does not abide by some timeline. Although the loss and pain will remain, the bereaved eventually learn to live again, gain control, and find meaning in their lives. But this doesn't happen overnight. This process could more aptly be described as recovery, as an ongoing, often lengthy, process. There is no way to measure our grief and comparing our mourning to others' is pointless.

According to therapist, Vivian Finlay, "There are, however, what are considered normal or abnormal ways of dealing with grief. Among the normal reactions are emotional outbursts, denial, anger, and disbelief. Abnormal reactions include denial to the point of pretending the loss simply didn't happen."

If the natural reactions to death are not allowed to manifest themselves, they will surface in other, potentially dangerous, ways. These symptoms may include but are not limited to: alcohol and drug abuse, repressed anger, or attempts to replace the loss by rushing into unjustified relationships. The grieving person has to face the loss alone. He or she will have to make personal decisions about how his or her particular path will progress. Eventually, the bereaved has to feel their own feelings and cry their own tears.

In addition, a big part of grieving has to do with our ability to communicate our feelings. We have to learn how to let go and express what we're experiencing or feeling inside.

According to research conducted by Dr. Ruth Fretts of Harvard University and Dr. Calvin Mackie, author of the book, *A View From the Roof,* women live longer than men for three main reasons:

1. *A woman will cry.* My mother's crying signified her decision to be honest with herself about her feelings. Crying is an emotional cleansing that is good for the soul.

2. *A woman will tell a friend her problems.* My mother called up her friends, relatives, and church members in order to have "sounding boards"—people whom she could bounce her emotions off of.

3. *A woman will give her problems to God.* My mother realized that regardless of how strong she was, she was incapable of bearing the weight of three dead children without the Power of God. When she tried to bear the weight alone, she remained immobile, for she could not move forward, so heavily burdened.

45

She finally came to the conclusion that she had God-sized problems.

Spare Not the Rod

Another such weight I carried, even into adulthood, was my anger at my parents' disciplinary techniques. Because my father worked so much, my mother was the primary disciplinarian. Her version of Christianity encouraged her to "spare not the rod," which meant I received whippings daily, with a belt, an extension cord, a shoe, a slab of bacon, or whatever else she could get her hands on the quickest. One beating tool that really stung was the water hose used to drain water from the washing machine into the sink. I used to take her whipping tools and throw them onto the roof of the abandoned building behind our house. When she went looking for something else and found one of my father's belts, I threw all of his belts onto the roof, too.

Although I was whipped for many different reasons, the primary motive was my education, or rather my refusal to participate in its realization. For example, I would get a bad report card or not get my report card signed by my parents on time. Or I would come home late because I didn't want to get a whipping after I had been bad in school. I would end up getting a whipping anyway because my mom didn't know where I was and whipped me for making her worry.

All my brothers and sisters seemed to have caught onto this old-school parenting technique and managed to avoid Mom's frequent whippings. But, Michael? No way! I was the black sheep of the family—the only one who insisted on getting in trouble.

Let it Burn

In addition to worrying about my mother's hand finding its way across my backside, I had to fear my older brothers. I was the youngest boy, and consequently the butt of many jokes—some far more cruel than funny. My brothers would wait until I was sound asleep to retrieve a big two-prong fork from the kitchen (the kind used for barbequing) or a humongous metal spoon. While I slept, they'd place one of the tools in a fire on the stove and let it marinate in the heat. When the spoon or fork was good and ready, they'd creep beside my sleeping body and lay the burning utensil on my arm. Waking up to that pain is indescribable. I cannot, even as a fully grown man, articulate the hurt it inspired. Stunned out of my six-year-old sleep, my first reaction was always to holler.

"Ahhhhhhh!"

And they'd stand above me like a collection of thieves who had not only stolen my sleep, but my peace as well.

"You gonna cry, ain't you? Look at him...he about to cry!"

With three sets of eyes on me and my "manhood" on the line, I couldn't give in to the quiver in my lip or the lump rising in my throat. I had to sit there and bear the pain, pretend to be a "man", and not even sniffle.

"I ain't gonna cry. I ain't gonna cry. It don't even hurt."

On my forearm, a black and red design rose. And remained.

To this day, I wear the physical marks of a spoon and a fork on my skin. It wasn't until recently that I was able to heal the emotional scars born at the hands of my brothers.

Don't Beat Me, Teach Me

My perception of the beatings was much different from my parents'. It seemed to me that there was always someone there to *beat* me for doing wrong, but no one there to *teach* me to do right. My father was overworked–too busy to talk to me about his expectations of and hopes for me. My mother was also overworked—tending the house and raising her many children. Looking back, I think my parents' aggressive discipline techniques were intended to instill fear in us.

As a result, I learned to respond to fear, and not love. The only way I could distinguish between the two was by what my parents *showed* me, not by what they *told* me. Therapist, Dr. Dan Baker, once stated, "Fear impels us to survive, and love enables us to thrive." When a child responds to fear and not love, he or she can suffer lasting, adverse reactions.

When my mother beat me, she would say, "Shut up all dat crying, 'fo' I give you something to cry about." So I would stop crying on the *outside*, but I would continue crying on the *inside*. Therefore, I never stopped crying. Although I would put on my "happy face" for people to see, I was still crying. Although I appeared to be joyful, I was still crying. Although tears were not rolling down my face, on the inside, I was still crying. Because I was not allowed to wash my face with tears to cleanse my soul's pain, I ended up self-destructing in an attempt to release that pain. Consequently, at an early age, I learned not to express my true feelings. I believe that children should never be told, "stop crying." If you've given your child a reason to cry, then they should cry. Crying is a symptom of genuine emotions that must be expressed authentically. If we tell our children to stop crying, then we're teaching them, subconsciously, to lie. Essentially, we're telling them to deny their feelings or to not feel at all. While I do not condone whining, I wholeheartedly support crying.

I believe I was raised just like many other African-American children, like children of any race, for that matter: through anger, hostility, and frustration. I'm not totally opposed to corporal discipline, but I believe when discipline is driven by reckless emotions it can very easily cross over into abuse. The anger, hostility, and frustration felt by many parents, particularly African-American parents, are often the driving forces behind verbal and physical discipline. Such unthinking methods of discipline are the very techniques prescribed by slave owners during slavery. For example, my mother would say things like, "I'm going to beat the black off you." This was a demeaning and derogatory phrase, used by the slave masters and overseers, which the African-American community inherited by default. We need to be cautious about using such phrases and realize the impact they will have on our families.

Primarily, we must avoid trying to solve spiritual problems with physical remedies. My parent's physical remedy was to beat me when I got into trouble, hoping that would make me stop. If beatings worked, I should have been an Angel. However,

49

the *insides* cannot be fixed from the *outside,* unless one is working on the *inside* from the *outside.* To fear and abuse only creates more problems. My solution to avoid getting beaten was to lie to my mother before she discovered the truth about me getting into trouble. Consequently, I got good at avoiding the *punishment,* but I never learned to solve the *problem.*

As a result of my many beatings, witnessing my sisters' deaths, and many other stresses too heavy for a child, I developed hatred toward mankind, even toward God, Himself. In fact, I used to curse God, "Where are You?" I would shout. "You're not real! I can't stand You! I hate You! You don't care about me!" I called Him every expletive I could think of. I couldn't understand what other people were talking about when they said, "God is good all of the time, and all of the time, God is good." I just couldn't understand why God would let a child go through all of that agony. As a result of my mistrust in God, whom I believed to be the Ruler of the Universe, how could I trust a mere man? I couldn't, so I grew to distrust people in general.

Hurt People, Hurt People

One of the most important lessons I've learned through self-discovery is that hurt people, hurt people. Because I was hurting inside, I hurt anyone who tried to love me. All I needed to hear were those magic words, "I love you," and it was on. The hurting could begin. An admission of love was an invitation for me to take advantage of an individual. Therefore, when people told me they loved me, I misused them. I had to commit the hurt before it was committed against me—all because love was reminiscent of my past, of those who supposedly loved me, but ultimately hurt me. On the other hand, I submitted to abuse; those who misused me garnered the most respect; I bowed down to them.

Until recently, I couldn't understand why I hurt so many of my girlfriends. It was because they tried to love me. And this wasn't just some ordinary hurt. *No.* I strived to hurt them beyond repair. I matched each effort to love me with a hurtful act. I was the type of guy who made women hate men.

I believe this is why so many African-American men hurt the loved ones they're with. Essentially, they're hurting inside. The thug image many of them portray is simply a façade. They're guarding their pain—pain they're afraid to share with their significant others. Many come from broken families, devoid of any positive male influence, or households rampant with drug-addicted relatives. Still, more are simply unsure about how to deal with the stressors of everyday life. This internal hurt is most evident when these injured men say nasty and hurtful things to their wives and girlfriends.

Ladies, it's important not to ignore these words. Do not pretend they don't hurt. The men will only come back with more hurtful blows; they'll try harder to let you know exactly how much pain they feel. Because they're hurting, they want the company they keep to also hurt.

Hurt people always try to get other people to feel what they're feeling. They like to convince themselves that their problems lie outside of themselves, rather than within. You have to watch out for this. They'll shift the blame to you, making you feel like it's your fault when really it isn't. Don't worry. They're sick. I was the type of man who caused women to pity themselves, to second guess themselves, to believe something was wrong with them, knowing all along it was me.

If this ever happens to you, begin asking the questions that will expose the truth: Why are you hurting? Who did this to you? Tell me what is really going on? What happened in your childhood that you're suppressing today?

If our approaches to disciplining our children are not corrected, the effects will be devastating—hurt children will continue to grow into hurt adults, and the world will be populated with individuals much like my young self. Our children will take advantage of people who tell them, "I love you," and look for ways to escape because of the uncomfortable feeling those words bring. Simultaneously, they'll succumb to people who abuse them, as if these people are their slave masters or overseers.

When we hurt inside, we must do away with the pain. Consequently, we hurt those around us. When we hurt, we hurt. Hurt people, hurt people. It is only when hurt people have been healed that they can love, and unselfishly, help people.

Grandma's Baby

One person whom I will never forget is my grandmother. She always showed me a lot of love, care, and concern. No matter how much I was perceived as the black sheep of the family, my grandmother always made me feel special. I think she knew I didn't get the love and affection I needed because our family was so large.

Whenever she came to Baltimore from North Carolina, she made sure to give me Ritz crackers while everyone else ate the regular old Saltines that were already in the cabinet. This special attention meant a lot to me. I was a child who never had the luxury of eating Ritz crackers because they were too expensive. Many poor folks in the ghetto ate Saltine crackers, which I considered to be the ghetto version of Ritz. But when Grandma came to town, she made sure that her Michael felt loved and appreciated.

This matter of crackers may seem like a small thing, but to a nine-year-old child in desperate need of attention, love, and affection, it meant the world. Looking back, I realize how important it is to pay close attention to the little things, because often it's the little things that make all the difference.

I can't remember my parents telling me I was loved or special. As a child, I was left to assume I was loved because my parents provided food, clothing, and a roof over my head. My family was, and still is, unaffectionate toward each other. Even today, my brothers and sisters don't say, "I love you" to each other like we should, which is a practice I look forward to beginning in the future.

Not until I was an adult did I understand the things my mother did to demonstrate her love for me. I had to assume she loved me because she never spoke the words. Children should never have to wonder if their parents love them. Many grandparents learn this lesson after their own children are grown. That's why they often try to show *more* love to their grandchildren than they did to their own children.

Case in point: Have you ever noticed a mother attempting to spank her children when the grandmother steps in and says, "Don't you put your hands on that baby!" Many grandmothers know about the importance of love. That's why whenever Grandma comes around she hugs and kisses her grandchildren, knowing how important affection is to a child. And when you visit her, she makes a special cake or pie just for her grandchild. Grandchildren know that whenever parents can't provide, they can look to Grandma.

But a grandmother who raises her grandchildren is often stricter than when she raised her own child. Grandmothers have learned from years of experience how important it is to be involved in a child's life. Research shows that adults who were raised by their grandparents say that their grandparents were strict, but that they later learned to appreciate the stern boundaries.

Like many other parents, my mother and father didn't know how to show their love. Few of us are masters at parenting, but through trial and error, we can learn the practical skills that our own parents never learned.

Healing with the Words, "I Love You!"

One of the many lessons I've learned from my parents' discipline techniques is that words are incredibly powerful. They can both hurt and heal. Children need to be told several times during the day that you love them. Some parents resist the idea of showing affection within the family. Some parents will even say, "My children know I love them." That may be true, but they need to hear it anyway. It reaffirms how much you care about them.

The three tender words, "I love you," are critical to a child's well being. We often take these words for granted, but I have never known a child to grow weary of hearing them. These words are nutritious. Without a consistent dose of these words, the very essence of a relationship between a parent and a child withers.

Don't Just Tell Me, Show Me

Your physical presence can also let children know you love them. As the child advocates say, "Children spell *love*, t-i-m-e." They will internalize that you do not love them if you do not spend time with them. If you are always in a hurry, your children will think you are too busy to pay attention to them. Unfortunately, many of us are reactive, rather than proactive when it comes to spending time with our children. We wait until it is too late and then try desperately to recover lost time.

Now Say It with Feeling

It's not what you say; it's how you say it. According to psychiatrist Katherine Wisner, the words we use make up only about ten percent of the communication process. Paralinguistics, the way we say the words, makes up forty percent. The remaining fifty percent consists of nonverbal features — what we do with our face, our body, and our hands as we speak.

The rhetorician Kenneth Burke once said that words don't have meaning unless you give them meaning. The difference between a reluctant "I love you" and an affectionate "I love you" is the difference between a confused child and a happy one.

Heal With A Hug

Many of us don't hug our children enough. They need to be hugged every day. Truth be told, you need it every day, too. Every day, before your children leave the house, give them a big hug, look them straight into their eyes, and tell them, "I love you." Trust me, it makes a big difference.

When you are hugged, your body releases chemicals called endorphins that make your body feel good. These endorphins increase your resistance to diseases and help to reduce pain. Never underestimate the power of a hug. Hugs are not only nice, they're necessary!

Help Carry the Load

You can help your children face everyday battles like peer pressure by communicating your love and understanding in words, through your physical presence, and with your hugs. As adults, we often underestimate the pressures children face in school and in the community. You can say something as simple as, "Look, I understand the amount of peer pressure you may experience in school, but I want you to know I love you to death. I know the stuff you face every day is big stuff, but I want you to know my love for you is way bigger than that." This kind of communication is critical. It helps your children carry the many burdens childhood promises. It also helps open the gates of communication—by initiating this sort of dialogue you let your children know you're available and willing to confront their problems with them. It may even determine whether they join a gang or end up addicted to drugs.

Now, Let it Go!

Regardless of what you've been through in your past, you must lay aside the weight that you carry. Many of us are still carrying the weight of the loss of a loved one, of an old grudge or an old relationship. Many of us just have unforgiving spirits. Today is a good time to remove what is on us, what is keeping us stagnant, so that we might run more swiftly and eventually soar.

On the other hand, what may be a weight to one person may not be a weight to another. Therefore, we must occasionally ask ourselves the question: "Is this a *wing*, or is it a *weight*?" The things we carry must be a *benefit*, not a *baggage*. We need to know whether a given idea, situation, or person helps us on our way to our destination, or slows us down. We can be so overwhelmed by failure that we just stop running. We just give up because giving up is easy. But we must be in the race for the long haul — in spite of the obstacles or the difficulties. Remember, you're not running a short dash; you're *running* a marathon, and it's called life!

Chapter 3

Troubles in My Way:

School Daze

"Education is our passport to the future, for tomorrow belongs to the people who prepare for it today."

—Malcolm X

trouble - *noun.* a state of distress, affliction, or difficulty within any given circumstance or situation.

Despite poverty, despite destitution, despite deprivation, my parents' commitment to my education stood resolute. My mother, an active and passionate member of the P.T.A. (Parent Teacher Association), never missed a report-card night or an after-school assembly. She was unswerving in her determination to be a force in my education, and I often imagined her looking over my shoulder, checking my assignments or questioning my behavior.

Even in a family as poor as ours, my parents always stressed the importance of doing well in school so that we could

59

get a "good education." My father was illiterate, which made him just as adamant as my mother about the importance of education. My mother made it clear, though, that if she ever had to come to the school to meet with a teacher, principal, or any other authority figure, it had better be because we'd done something good. This rule seemed to work well for my brothers and sisters, but once again, not for me.

Class Clown

If you asked any of my teachers what kind of student I was, they would all say that I gave them a lot of hell. From kindergarten through high school, I kept my mother busy going back and forth to the school on my behalf. Far too often, my mom was called to rectify some infraction of mine, some breach of school rules. She would storm through the school building's doors with me in mind, and march back through them with me in tow. I just couldn't seem to shake my mischievous behavior.

I always wanted to be the class clown, because being disruptive was a way to camouflage my illiteracy. I also wanted to be the center of attention at all times, no matter the cost, because I wanted to be a part of the "in crowd." That way, the attention would be on my behavior and not my poverty. As a consequence, I consistently received failing grades.

I was sent home almost every day for acting out in school, and with each dismissal, I knew to expect a beating. This made my walk home the longest walk ever. The four blocks between the school and my house swelled to fourteen. And gradually, a five-minute walk turned to a five-hour stroll. I couldn't stomach the thought of my mother's greeting — short on hello, and long on whipping — so I slowed my pace and let my feet drag where they would have usually strutted. Suddenly, the neighborhood was more colorful, more interesting, and needed to be meticulously viewed. The beating, despite my tourist-style walk, always awaited my arrival.

Usually my mom had already received a phone call outlining my behavior before I even reached the house's threshold. And as soon as I walked through the door, her whipping tool was upon me and my body was swelling with welts. Yet, nothing — not my mom's belt across my behind, not my dad's words slapped angrily against my ears, not my teachers' looks of disdain when I entered the classroom — deterred my actions. My behavior wouldn't change for nearly two decades.

Michael the Menace

My third-grade teacher, Mrs. Sanders, collected notes on my disobedient episodes and stored them where they could be retrieved easily–she seemed to keep my disciplinary history in her front pocket and recovered it whenever we interacted. I could never look forward to a new day with Mrs. Sanders, because for her I remained the same Michael from yesterday — a menace. Each morning she greeted me with a drawn out "Good... morning..." and faithfully affixed her assumptions and disgust to that salutation. And while I claimed the vast majority of her classroom disruptions, the title, "menace," could not be shaken – I had to wear it storm or shine.

One particular morning exemplified this branding. My

mom was downstairs in a parent/teacher conference to discuss some trouble I had gotten myself into just a couple of days prior. Mrs. Sanders was writing the day's assignment on the chalkboard. While her back was turned, my classmates began shooting spitballs across the room. Mrs. Sanders stopped writing and looked around to see who was causing all the commotion. She assumed it was me, but on that particular day, it wasn't. I had just gotten into trouble a couple of days before and my hind parts were still sore from that whipping.

She then pulled my long disciplinary history from her front pocket and, without even turning from where she stood, she yelled, "Michael, why are you shooting those spitballs across my room?"

I replied in a shocked voice, "It wasn't me, Mrs. Sanders!"

She said, "It was you! Now, get over here!"

I sauntered through the aisles of the classroom with my thrift-store jeans and my brand-new, K-Mart-fabulous shirt. I remember that shirt fondly. It had colorful stripes and a red collar. It instantly became my favorite because it was store-bought, and it was so seldom I received brand-new clothes. I was unusually clean on that day, too. I was looking just as I was, half thrift store, and half brand new.

I trotted over to Mrs. Sanders with the welts from the beating still stinging my backside, and with absolute certainty that I would be believed. After all, my mom sat only one floor below Ms. Sanders' classroom in a parent/teacher conference. Surely, Mrs. Sanders knew that I was sharp enough not to disturb her class while my mom was downstairs at a parent/ teacher conference. I was unruly, not stupid.

Mrs. Sanders grabbed me by the collar and yanked me so hard that she ripped the collar off my shirt. Boy was I upset! She uttered those famous, verbally abusive words that so many teachers were notorious for using back then: "You must not get enough attention at home!" That saying was commonplace inside our classroom walls, and it served a dual injustice: to silence the child, but also to humiliate him.

Although she may have been right, given the size of my family and our circumstances, I felt like she had no right to say that. To make matters worse, the entire class burst out laughing. Instantly, the tables were turned. I had gone from class clown to laughingstock. I had been both violated and humiliated.

Back then, the intercom system was set up so that teachers could call from the classroom to the main office. Mrs. Sanders, knowing my mom was in the building, walked over to the intercom and called the office where my mom was having the parent/ teacher conference.

"Mrs. Miller," she strongly advised, "you need to come get your son and teach him some home training."

Mrs. Sanders then ushered me out of her classroom and demanded that I go to the first floor and find my mother. Needless to say, my mom was quite embarrassed and wore a bright flush all across her face and neck. She started on a rampage of her own—waving her hands and arms in a blind fury—when she saw me. Rather than question my behavior, she called Mrs. Sanders "sassy." She took me by the hand and hurriedly walked me back to Mrs. Sanders' classroom, all the while going off. She kept saying Mrs. Sanders was being too "sassy." She seethed over what had just occurred, and I listened with a clamped-shut mouth.

That's Not Even A Word

As she frequently did back then, my mom threw in a couple of made-up words, "I ain't gonna have no *pristalistic* woman put her hands on my son. She must have lost her mind! Dat shirt cost me three dollars and ninety-nine cents. We don't have a bunch of money to be *frubalistically* throwing away. I ain't gonna have nobody disturb me in an *innoventabuttous* manner while I'm in the parent/teacher conference. I got neck-bones, black-eye peas, and collard greens on da stove, and now she gon' make me late. Shoot! I've been nice to her since day one, and I ain't gonna have it no mo'!"

By the time we reached the top of the stairs, we were breathless, but we continued at the same rate to Mrs. Sanders' classroom door. My mom opened the door to signal Mrs. Sanders to step out into the hallway. She then assumed her humble Christian pose: She tilted her head slightly to the side and laced her fingers together as if to begin a prayer. From her mouth came a perfectly soft voice (completely unlike the riotous one she displayed during her irate trek up the stairs), "Mrs. Sanders, excuse me, could you please step outside the door?"

Mrs. Sanders joined us with an annoyed look on her face. Then, my mom let her have it.

"There are several things 'dat I would like to speak to you

about dis afternoon. Number one, don't nobody put their hands on my son but me, okay? Dat shirt cost me three dollars and ninety-nine cents. And don't you evah call where I am and disrespect me again! You unda'stand? You make sure dis is the last d@mn time you evah get sassy wit me. But I'll tell you one d@mn thang. Call down there again and see what happens, I dare you!"

Whenever my mom was around teachers and she couldn't exactly express her point, she'd be compelled to make up words in order to sound intelligent. The teachers would look at her strangely, trying to figure out the meanings of the odd words rather than focusing on what she was trying to say. For example, she was calling Mrs. Sanders "sassy," which was commonly used around my household when we kids talked back to a grown up or acted above ourselves, but what my mom really meant was that Mrs. Sanders was being 'sarcastic.'

Things might have remained purely verbal and nearly orderly had Ms. Sanders not belittled my mom. My mom, in an effort to appear intelligent, said, "And don't you get sassy and *sissyfalicous* with me, young lady. Oh, no!"

Mrs. Sanders responded in a very condescending voice, "Hey, that's not even a word, Mrs. Miller." Before the smirk had settled on Mrs. Sanders' lips, my mom was on top of her, beating her down on the floor, much like one of her own children!

I immediately ran to the main office to tell someone that my mom, a devoted PTA member, was stomping my third-grade teacher, like a mere bug, just one floor above. By the time I arrived at the main office, I was totally out of breath. I gasped,

"Huh, huh, huh, excuse me, my mom, ah, my mom, is upstairs…"

Before I could finish, the school secretary said, "Huh?"

Trying to catch my breath, I said, "Ah, my mom is upstairs, beating…"

"You will have to wait your turn," she interrupted. "Now, get somewhere and sit down!"

I said to myself, *What?* The secretary's refusal to recognize the fear in my shaking voice and sweating face infuriated me. Since she wanted me to wait, I would wait. I sat and waited for ten long minutes while my mom was upstairs, beating the living hell out of Mrs. Sanders!

When the news finally got back to the main office, the faculty, teachers, and administrators came from all over the building to break up the fight. Back then, they didn't have school police officers in elementary schools, so no one could control my mom. She was in the middle of the hallway, yelling, "Yeah, call the police! I ain't scared of no police! Call the police!"

My mom had a very good relationship with the principal, a White man named Mr. Walpert. He was a polite man who respected my mom for raising nine children (all of whom went through Gilmore Elementary School) while being actively involved in the PTA. He frequently drove her home after the PTA meetings, instead of letting her walk home in the dark.

When the police finally arrived to lock my mom up, they started to manhandle her despite the fact that she made no attempt to resist arrest.

Meanwhile, I was crying and shouting, "Get your hands off of my mama!"

Mr. Walpert hastily intervened, "Now, wait just one cotton-picking minute, buddy!" he said to the policeman who was about to handcuff her, "Don't you guys dare disrespect and put handcuffs on her! And stop mishandling her like she's some criminal! She is a lady, a decent, law-abiding citizen who is actively involved in the PTA meetings here and has sent her nine children through this school! Now, take those handcuffs off her immediately and treat her like the person she is — a lady! So, respect her as one!"

I will never forget that moment. I was delighted at what Mr. Walpert had said. The administrators were amazed. The cops were confounded. The teachers were traumatized. Here was a White man, of some stature, adamantly standing up for the civil rights of a Black woman. Immediately, the foyer fell silent. The cops obeyed Mr. Walpert's commands. One of them got on his radio and requested a policewoman to come down from the precinct, which was only one block away. She arrived quickly, taking the handcuffs off my mom and putting finger-cuffs on her instead, and then she escorted my mom out of the building to the police cruisers.

I stood there in the foyer, crying loud as a baby, thinking I would never see my mother again. Filled with anger and frustration, I despised everyone around me and blamed them for my mom being taken away. As the administrators tried to calm me down, I retaliated with mean and hateful words. "Get your d@mn hands off of me heffa. I hate ya'll. Ya'll make me sick...I can't stand this place..." I wanted them to feel what I was feeling.

I sat in the main office asking myself, *What happened? My church-going, spirit-filled, Christian mother had lost her mind and beat up my teacher!*

It wasn't until about an hour later that I finally calmed down, with the assistance of Mr. Walpert. He assured me that everything would be okay. And, for some strange reason, I believed him. He called my father on his job and asked him to come pick me and my brothers and sisters up from school.

While we were home, I waited all night long, wishing and hoping for my mother to return from jail. I must have cried a million tears waiting for her.

"Michael, stop all dat crying," my father said. "Yo' mama gonna be just fine! Y'all chil'ren need to learn how to have some faith. God didn't bring us dis far to leave us now. Shoot! If it wasn't fo' the Lawd, we wouldn't have all the thangs we got now!"

I said to myself, "But daddy, we ain't got nothing!"

Then my father walked away, singing one of his favorite gospel songs for inspiration, "If it had not been/ for the Lawd on my side/ tell me where would I be? (Whoa yeah!)/ Where would I be?" He then left the house and returned home with my mother late that evening. I had thought she would never get out of jail, but ultimately I was relieved of my misery.

Following the fight between my mom and Mrs. Sanders, my brothers and sisters and I had to be transferred to Matthew A. Henson Elementary. I instantly fell in love with my new school. After lunch, we had recess and played outside for half an hour. We ate with stainless-steel forks and spoons, and porcelain plates and trays–not the plastic spoon-forks and Styrofoam plates we used at our previous school. Of course, the transition was a bit difficult because my friends weren't there, but I got used to it.

During the first week of school, I immediately made a name for myself. I felt like I had to act out to fit in with the "cool" kids. I was disruptive in class and picked on other students all day.

Meanwhile, my mom was facing a ten-year sentence for assault and battery. She walked boldly into the courtroom without a public defender or a hired attorney, steadfast in her faith in God and confident that she could represent herself. She just quoted one of her usual adages, "He's a lawyer in the courtroom." Even though my mother had faith in God and solely depended on Him to get her through her trial, I didn't. I sat in the courtroom, petrified that she would go to jail.

When it was finally time for my mother to approach the courtroom podium, the judge said to her, "I would send you to jail, but I'm afraid because you have so many children. I wouldn't want them to be raised without a mother." Then he asked her, "Mrs. Miller, are you sure you can raise all of these children?"

My mom replied with certainty, "Yes."

So, the judge gave her one-year of probation.

Needless to say, I was overjoyed by the judge's decision.

My Mama Prayed for Me!

After that incident, things began to change. My mother finally realized that she had to try a different approach for disciplining me. Evidently, the beatings just weren't working. The only method of punishment my mother knew was the one that had been passed down to her from generation to generation: frequent beatings for frequent misbehavior. By the time I was in middle school, she was getting tired of beating me and receiving no results, so she finally looked to the hills from which comes her help, God.

One day I was sent home from middle school for fighting a classmate and cursing out a teacher. I just knew I was going to get a beating. When I arrived home, my mom greeted me with a mighty stream of tears, pouring down her face. She took me by the hand and led me to the foot of her bed. She was so drained, so fed up with my ways, and disgusted with trying to beat some sense into me. Her confidence in her disciplining methods had wavered and was taking a toll on her mental and physical health. Her self-esteem had depleted. She had no choice but to turn to God. She had taken me as far as she could. Enough was enough. It was now time to impart the power of prayer.

Still holding my hand, she told me to kneel with her at the foot of her bed. I didn't know what was going on. Tears continued to roll from her eyes, and she looked puzzled and confused as she cried out, "Peace, be still!"

I had caused her so much pain and anguish that she cried out loud and clear, "Father, I stretch out my hands to Thee, for there is no other help that I know!" She mourned and wept, "God, if I ever needed You before, I sure do need You right now! Lawd, this one child, Michael, just can't seem to get right."

It had only been about ten minutes, but it seemed as if we had prayed for an hour. My mother went into her metaphysical state where she walked around the room, lifting up her hands and shouting, "Thank ya, Jesus! Thank ya! I claim this child in the name of Jesus!" Then she shifted in the middle of her prayer and talked to the devil. She said, "devil, I rebuke you! Get out of my house!"

I knelt there, just wondering when it was going to end. She returned to her knees and to praying, squeezing my hand even tighter shouting, "In the name of Jesus, I claim victory over my son, right now! God, for every sin he has committed, I cast it into the sea of forgiveness! I claim victory over his misbehaving in school! Whatever he can't get right, make it right! Whatever seems to have grabbed hold of 'im, loosen it, Lawd!" She finally closed the prayer with her seal of approval, "Let the words of my mouth, and the meditation of my heart be always acceptable in thy sight. Amen!"

That moment was very spooky to me. My mother was a firm believer in the power of prayer, but I was confused by her intentions. That was the first and only time she took me by the hand to pray with me. After that, she stopped giving me whippings and became a little more lenient with me. I will never forget that day for the rest of my life.

But Does Prayer Change Things?

On one hand, my mother's strange behavior imparted a lesson she could never teach me through physical punishment. I understood with that passionate prayer that she would rely on her spirituality to finish the race of raising me.

On the other hand, I felt her prayer had been in vain, because I didn't change immediately. I got into trouble, again and again, for my disruptive conduct in school. I remember questioning my mother's new discipline tactics. When I came home, she started talking to me, instead of beating me. I challenged her by saying, "You see, Mama, that prayer you said for me last week didn't even work."

Her response was, "He may not come when you want Him to come, but He's an on-time God. *Yes, He is!*"

Days turned into weeks and weeks turned into months and I didn't see any change in my behavior for the next ten years. I asked myself, *"Does prayer really change things, or is it all a hoax?"*

Hold on to that thought....*To be continued.*

To Be Popular or to Be Smart

Choosing popularity over intellect costs a high price: failure. My teachers complained constantly about my low math and reading skills. To improve my math skills, my mom made me memorize the entire multiplication table found on the inside cover of my black-and-white composition book. Everyday, she and I recited the table, until I finally memorized it—all the way through twelve times table.

Because of my disruptive behavior and illiteracy, the teachers labeled me. I remember overhearing them say they wanted to put me in Special Education, which was called D.E.C. (Department of Exceptional Children) back then. Kids would tease students in D.E.C. classes, saying D.E.C. stood for "Dumb Educated Children." I would rhetorically ask myself, *"How can you be both dumb and educated all at the same time? I guess kids say the darnedest things."*

The learning disability labels the teachers thought were appropriate for me were LD and ED, meaning "Learning Disabled" and "Emotionally Disturbed." Marian Wright Edelman, a social reformer, once said, "Parents have become so convinced educators know what is best for children that they forget that they, themselves, are really the experts." My mother held the same belief. Regardless of my hyperactive behavior and poor performance in class, she fought those stigmas and rejected those terms by saying things like, "Nothing is wrong wit' you, Michael. Dem teachers up at dat school don't know you." My mom, who was an ardent biblical scholar, began to quote Scriptures and remind me once again, "Through God, all things are possible." She always knew just what to quote from the Bible just when I needed it.

Dr. Jawanza Kunjufu, who wrote, To Be Popular or to Be Smart, said that before the fourth grade, the average African-American child has the intellectual aptitude to do well in math and in science. But by the time they actually get to the fourth grade, they are reading two grade levels below where they should be. This is not because African-Americans are intellectually limited, but because many of us make the conscious decision to be *popular* rather than *smart*.

Many young people make the same mistake I did—choosing popularity over intelligence. At some point, each young person has to ask, "Do I want to continue to be *popular* or do I want to be *smart*?" Indeed, this problem is not limited to the young, African-American population; this is a problem with young people in general. So, if you want to make an impression on your grades, "Show the teachers your MINDS, not your BEHINDS!"

Middle-School Gang Wars

After elementary school, I went to Lemmel Middle School–a very tough and disruptive environment that encouraged student failure. Gang fights were an every day occurrence. They occurred on the bus to school, during school, and after school. It was normal for a seventh or eighth-grade student to bring to school a .22, a .32, a .38 automatic, or whatever type of weapon they could get their hands on. When guns weren't available, students carried knives to protect themselves. Because it was the only way to survive, I, too, developed the mentality of a juvenile delinquent.

Many of us spent our time in woodshop class carving sticks to fight with or fashioning hard plastic knives to use as daggers. All of this was done while the teacher's back was turned, tending to the other disruptive students in the class. Lemmel Middle School often rivaled with Frederick Douglass

High School. Lemmel students would go to Douglass High School to fight and vice versa. Toward the end of my sixth-grade year, I was expelled from Lemmel Middle School and sent to Calverton Middle School to finish the year. I didn't know it then, but God had a plan for me. He was ordering my steps.

A Father at Fourteen

I lost my virginity while attending Calverton. It happened on my fourteenth birthday with my girlfriend, whose name was Candy. She and I were the same age. It was evident that I had a sweet tooth for her, because I came around her house looking for her every chance I got. One afternoon, Candy's foster-mother, Mrs. May, walked her to my house to talk to my parents. I was in my mom's room at the front of the house, watching the scene and gauging their reactions.

My mother answered the door and assumed her normal Christian pose: an erect back, arms resting politely at her side, chin lifted just enough to signify her pride in her uprightness.

"Hello, may I help you?" she asked.

The woman at the door was tight-lipped and determined. She said, "Good evening. My name is Mrs. May, and I just want you to know that your son, Michael, well, he got my foster-daughter pregnant."

Those words hit my mother good, right between the eyes. She tensed and made fists of her hands. Just as she had done with my third-grade teacher, Mrs. Sanders, she quickly came to my defense. Only this time, I really was at fault.

"Oh, no! Not my son!" she said, fighting back tears. "You

see, my son goes to Zion Hill Missionary Baptist Church every Sunday, where the Reverend Goode is the very fine pastor! He is a child of God...yes, he is. My son is saved, baptized, and washed in the blood of the Lamb!"

She stopped to breathe and take in Mrs. May's words. The two women looked at each other. Obviously, neither wanted the words to be true, but one, Mrs. May, was much closer to believing them than the other.

"Besides, my son is only fourteen years old, you know?"

My mother started up again, this time seasoning her talk with those made-up words so comfortable in her mouth, "There is no way my son could have fertilaciously and impregnatatiously fertilized a baby into your dawta. He is just a baby, Mrs. May! He's still wet behind the ears."

Mrs. May replied, "Mrs. Miller, your son, Michael, ain't all what he is cracked up to be. There were plenty of times when I had to run him away from my door, because he was around my house so much. He was always coming around, looking for Candy."

"Now hold on there, Mrs. May," my mother interjected. "I just don't know how true that is. One thang I know about my son is that if he wanted some candy, he would've earned his own money to buy his own candy. He would've went round the corner to the market to carry them people's groceries. He would've pumped some gas at the gas station, or cut somebody's grass to get his own money to buy his own candy — 'fore he went begging you for some."

Had things not been so serious, Mrs. May might've

laughed at my mother's confusion. But things were serious, and Mrs. May was growing impatient.

"Oh, Mrs. Miller, you don't understand..." she began.

Before the woman could explain that "Candy" was her daughter's name and not a lollipop or ten-cent taffy, my mother interrupted her and talked over her words with bigger, purely invented ones, "Oh, no, I understand, all right. I understand y'all trying to put a *conspiracitation* on my son. That's what I understand! Y'all trying to set him up, saying that Michael *fertilaciously impregnatized* yo' dawta! But that shall not be the revelation here today. *Thus saith the Lord, thy God!* Because the Bible says" — and here she closed her eyes to let the mighty spirit fill her — "Touch not my anointed and do my child no harm!" She punctuated those words with a slight lift of her already-raised chin, and there she remained — chin raised, eyes shut so tightly that no light could seep in.

"Mrs. Miller" — Mrs. May ignored those closed eyes — "please relax. You see, I'm not talking about the kind of candy that children eat. My daughter, Mrs. Miller, my daughter's name is Candy!"

My mother let those words settle on her. They must have held meaning, because she peeled back her eyelids and held her tongue still. She regrouped and allowed Mrs. May to have her say. After the woman had said her piece, my mother cleared her throat and smoothed her dress with the very hands that only seconds before had been fists.

"I'm sorry, Mrs. May," she said. "I'm so sorry. Well, okay, then. I'll be sure to tell his daddy when he gets home."

For every word my mother invented, my father stuttered three or four. When the frustration was too big, when it bubbled within him and made a mess of his thoughts, no one, not even himself, could understand what he was saying. And learning that I'd gotten a girl pregnant at fourteen was one of those times.

"Hey, Micka, Mmm-mm-Macka!" My name was a bundle of confusion on his tongue. "Ma-ma-ma-ma-Macka, ge-ge-ge-get down here, r-r-r-r-ret now!"

As soon as I came downstairs, I responded, "Ye-ye-ye-ye-yes, sir?"

My father instantly began to chew me out, "Now wha-wha-wha-what in da hell you go off and, uh, get some gal pregnant fo'?" He paused to take a breath and started up again, "I tell, I tell ya, I tell ya, boy, I tell ya, ta-ta-ta-tell ya." He paused, took a breath to sigh "Phew!" and then wiped the sweat from his forehead. "You ain't got two cents worf of good sense! I tell ya one thang, ya gonna get a job and work. You ain't si-si-si-sittin' around da house. Ya gittin' da hell outa here. I tell you, boy, ya ca-ca-can't, can't, can't, can't do nothing right. Every time I turn around, ya always into something, ya knotty-headed rascal! Why can't ya do good like da rest of da chil'ren?"

Contemplating Fatherhood

After the lecture from my father, I knew having a baby meant serious business. My father didn't believe in abortion. He had taken on the challenge of raising his twelve children. Nor did the idea cross my mind, possibly because I was still a child myself.

We were fourteen-year-old babies about to have a baby–a circumstance neither of us was mentally, emotionally, educationally, or financially prepared for. The thoughts running through my head scared and confused me: How do you take care of a baby? What am I supposed to do if it cries? Where is the money going to come from? How do you love a child? Do you beat them when they do wrong? It was emotionally draining just attempting to answer those questions. I was carrying an adult load on a child's back, and the weight was too much for me to bear. In fact, neither of us took it seriously enough to prepare ourselves. I remember being very afraid. My solution was to run away from my responsibilities. Like my father, I always wanted a better way for my family, but I didn't want to be "a daddy at a distance" as he had been, or struggle to earn a living as he had done. I wanted to be there to watch my future children grow. I wanted to show my children that I valued them, not just with words but also with actions and a physical presence. As the pressure mounted, I gradually stopped wanting to be around Candy. Suddenly, I didn't have a sweet tooth for her anymore. Moreover, I realized I couldn't provide for our son, so rather than be a failure, I walked away.

Toward the end of her pregnancy, when she was visiting my house, I finally confronted her and told her exactly how I felt, "Candy, this is too stressful for me. What am I gonna do? I don't have a job, and we still live with our parents. I hardly see you because you've moved to the other side of town. So, I think it's best that we just break up."

She looked at me sadly and said, "Why would you do

something like this? Don't you think it's hard on me, too? Michael, I don't want to lose you."

I responded childishly, "I don't want to lose you, either, Candy, but hey, a man gotta do what a man gotta do."

Her sister called her, "Candy, c'mon. It's time to go home. Besides, he aint even worth it!" As she walked away, she looked at me in confusion, knowing she would have to carry the bulk of the adult load by herself, without my assistance as a father or as a boyfriend.

I just stood there hurt, lost, confused, and holding back tears. I could barely take care of myself with the help of my mother. How could I take care of a family? Still, I felt I was leaving behind a friend whom I could talk to about anything. Now I had to bear life's burdens alone and Candy had to bear parenthood in the same manner, all because I was scared of being a father, scared of being responsible for a life other than my own. I ran the streets and taught myself how to survive.

Failing as a Father

Of all of the things I've regretted in my life, I regret most not being a father to my son during his infancy. After Dévon was born, I continued to hang out on the streets with the wrong crowd. I often felt bad, knowing I was running away from my responsibility, but I had many outside influences encouraging me to do so, and very few people to show me how to do better. The people around me were incapable of modeling effective parenting. Besides, I couldn't learn how to be a father from any of them. They would often deny their children by saying, "Dat ain't my baby." My priorities as a fourteen-year-old child were running the streets, hanging on the corners, and partying. As a result, I failed as a father to Dévon, and I failed as a boyfriend to Candy.

Even though Candy and I were no longer a couple, my father expected me to be a responsible parent to my son. He believed, firmly, that if you have a baby, you take care of it. But because my father worked most of the time, he couldn't monitor my parenting. He would come home and ask, "Boy, did you go see your son today?"

I would respond with a lie, "Yes, sir!"

When Dévon was about a year old, Candy began bringing him to see me. After that, my dad would go and get him occasionally and bring him to the house. Usually, I wasn't home. When I was, I didn't know what to do, what to feel, or what to think. I wanted to be a father and show my son the love and affection a father should, but I didn't know how. Instead, I hit the streets and after a while that lifestyle became second nature. Besides my father's earnest attempts, there weren't many loving fathers around to inspire me, none that I was conscious of, anyway.

Unfortunately, Dévon wasn't the only child I neglected during my early teen years. When I was seventeen, I got my girlfriend, Nikki, pregnant. I knew I was the father of her child, but I responded as usual, "That ain't my baby!" She, too, felt the wrath of my juvenile and insensible ways. I was actually present when my daughter, Brianna, was born, which made me a little more attached to her. However, it was after she was born that my failure-as-a-father rampage created havoc for me to see her as often. Nikki couldn't risk leaving her with me because of my impulsive, juvenile behavior.

I'm Holding Her Hostage

I've heard it once stated that the father of a daughter is nothing but a high-class hostage. Well, I just happened to take mine a step further. I decided to actually hold my daughter hostage, refusing to never let her go back home to her mother. You see, from witnessing and being there since Brianna's birth, I built a special bond with her and I was determined to never let her go. She represented the purity of love and attachment I'd yearned for, and I was determined to keep hold of what I'd been missing.

One day I was high on marijuana and left Brianna in the house with my nine-year-old nephew. I told him to watch her while I went to hang out in downtown Baltimore. Nikki called the house and soon discovered I had left. When I happened to call her, she told me she was on her way to my house with the police. I rushed back to the house and got there just before Nikki and the police arrived. The police banged on my door and hollered, "Mr. Miller, open the door, NOW!" I took puff after puff of the weed I was smoking, and responded, "You can keep on knockin', but ya' can't get in!" Then I started singing right behind the door, so they could hear me, "I shot the sheriff, but I didn't shoot the deputy!" Meanwhile, my newborn baby was crying from the relentless bangs on the door. After about five more minutes, I opened the door and let them take her away. Again, I was a neglectful, unsupportive father.

I continued to deem the streets more important than my children. I thought giving them a little money here and there qualified as sufficient care. But money was not what they really needed. More than anything else, they needed my *attention*, not my *cash*.

Many fathers believe that as long as they provide their children with the basic necessities, they're adequate parents. They also have the misconception that as long as they pay child support, they're doing their part. But raising a child means more than providing food and shelter or paying the bills. It means providing emotional support, and above all, providing love.

The Truth is in the Youth   My parents, church family, & dad's side ; some teachers

In the words of the old African proverb, "It takes a village to raise a child." But when the village is crazy, it produces crazy children. Dr. Jawanzaa Kunjufu concurs that young people have a story to tell, if only adults will listen.

When he asked teenagers, "What do your parents and teachers tell you about school?" they responded, "Get a good education and work." When he asked them how they felt about those comments, they answered, "Get a good education for what? Work hard for who?" They also want to know the relevance, the need, or the reason for each lesson.

Dr. Kunjufu believes young African-Americans stopped asking questions and began cheating when they found out the most important objective in school was not learning but receiving good grades. He further claims that our youth have determined

83

that securing employment is based more on *who* you know rather than *what* you know.

According to Dr. Kunjufu, young African-Americans see numerous ways to make money without getting a good education or working hard. He also notes that young people believe, "I'm going to be like Michael Jordan, Allen Iverson, Jay-Z, or Beyonce," without an appreciation of what it requires to become anything. They are motivated to *be* great, but not motivated to *become* great. Becoming great requires discipline, sacrifice, time management, vision, patience, and above all else, work. He attributes this misconception to young people watching "instant success" stories on television, instead of observing how their parents earn a living.

Just like adults, children will encounter obstacles that may block their paths. Help your children understand that these roadblocks are a part of life and that they can be overcome.

Adults, too, need to learn this lesson. Everyone would succeed in every attempt and win every race if there were no obstacles. Your job is to be persistent and work through them. If you find only a few along the way, chances are you're not really challenging yourself. If you want to experience the feeling of sweet success, make your goal a challenging one!

Chapter 4

Shun Not the Struggle:
Face it, it's God's Gift

"If there is no struggle there is no progress. Those who profess to favor freedom and yet depreciate agitation, are men who want crops without plowing up the ground, they want rain without thunder and lightening. They want the ocean without the awful roar of its many waters.... Power concedes nothing without demand. It never did and it never will."

—Frederick Douglass

struggle - *verb.* to make great efforts, to labor hard, to strive, or contend forcibly under difficult conditions

Rather than accept my struggles as necessary parts of life, I avoided them. I preferred escape and tried to find easy ways out of any difficult situation. In my early teens, I was a delinquent and according to most, one who would never amount to much. I would smoke marijuana every chance I got—first thing in the morning, at lunchtime, and all night. My friend, Nate, and I used to smoke marijuana every day before going to school. Nate's parents were marijuana dealers and kept a healthy supply in their basement. Every morning, Nate and I would steal a couple of fistfuls and stuff them in sandwich bags. We'd be so high we could barely keep our eyes open. Walking through the classroom doors with clothes drowned in that very recognizable scent, we had no intentions of learning. We couldn't do much more than laugh or scratch our heads, let alone concentrate. I can't imagine how much time we wasted getting high on superficial chemicals, rather than accepting the education being given to us, questing for some knowledge, or something more from life. It was ridiculous.

Same Hook, Different Bait

I found myself justifying my marijuana addiction by telling myself smoking marijuana was not as bad as smoking crack–as if it's alright to smoke marijuana. What's the difference between smoking marijuana and smoking crack? The difference is time. It takes a little longer to kill yourself with marijuana.

People who gossip think they're better off than people who shop to numb their emotions. Shopaholics think they're better than sexaholics; sexaholics think they're better than alcoholics; alcoholics think they're better than heroin addicts; and heroin addicts think they're better than crack addicts. Crack cocaine addicts live at such a low level they don't think they're better than anybody. Addiction is the same hook with different bait.

It's not the trap that killed the rat; it was the love of cheese. Just as the rat took the chance of dying to get the cheese, I took the chance of smoking marijuana and killing myself for the high.

But smoking marijuana wasn't the biggest problem I wrestled with. I was also stealing cars and hanging out on the street corners with my friends when I was supposed to be in school. Toward the end of my seventh-grade year at Calverton, I was arrested for breaking into the new condominiums being built not far from my neighborhood. As a result, I was sent to the Charles Hickey Juvenile Detention Center. Because of my age, my parents were the only ones allowed to pick me up from the police station, and once they did, I had to stay home until my trial date. But, my dad warned me that if I ever got into trouble again, he would not come down to get me.

"Ba-ba-boy, if-if-if ya git locked up and go to jail, you will stay there — cause' I ain't coming to git ya!"

Did I believe him? No.

One day, while I was waiting for another trial date and skipping school, I was caught throwing rocks at cars coming down the highway. I was trying to make the cars crash into each other. A police officer spotted me and chased me into an alley where several police cars blocked me in. After placing me under arrest, they called my parents. My father told them he wasn't coming to get me, so I was taken to the juvenile detention center. This time my tenure at Charles Hickey lasted much longer—the bulk of my seventh-grade year. When I was released, I was even more frustrated and furious than before. Rather than having learned to respect the law at Charles Hickey, I'd picked up even more schemes for surviving life in the streets. My fellow inmates had been my teachers. I became even more devious and started getting into even more trouble.

Eighth grade came around, and after several suspensions, I was expelled from Calverton Middle School for fighting. I was sent to Harlem Park Middle School. On the third day at my new school, I got into another fight because somebody got smart with a friend who lived around the corner from me. Harlem Park didn't waste any time with me. I was expelled immediately. The school board ultimately sent me back to Lemmel Middle School, where I finally made it to the finish line: I graduated from eighth grade. I had to graduate as a result of social promotion since I hadn't done much work.

Borrowing the Benz

My father was a working man. He never knew the sun he worked so hard — he was up and working before it rose and still breaking his back when it set. Because he held two jobs, he wandered home at the end of each day drunk with exhaustion, desperately looking for somewhere to lie down. When his head finally hit some surface — a pillow, a couch cushion, or even the back of a chair — he said, "Good night" to the world and slept like the dead. You could hear him throughout the entire house, "Sn-nooock, cl-cl-cloookk ... sn-nooock, cl-cl-cloookk." He couldn't help himself. He had sleep apnea, which stole his breath temporarily.

Each night, as he fought to sleep and breathe all at once, his brand-new, money-green, 1987, S-Class, Mercedes Benz sat outside, collecting dust. Well, not exactly ... he had an old, beat-up, '77 Chevy Impala, the color of peas, which I called a

Mercedes Benz. It sat before our house many nights, unbothered, ignored, waiting for him to regain consciousness and come warm its seats in the early-morning hours. Until, of course, I discovered its worth.

In my sixteen-year-old confidence, I began "borrowing" the "Benz." I'd cruise the city for two or three hours at a time, with the seat leaned so far back I could barely see the cars ahead of me, let alone the road. With the radio turned on "deaf" and in the welcome company of my friends, I drove from one side of town to the next. I was a thief, but my antics could neither hurt nor worry my father — he was sleeping.

As soon as he stopped breathing, in-between his snores, I'd sneak up beside him, find his pants, reach down to the lint-filled bottom of his pocket, mute the keys resting there with my hand, and then flee. Before he resumed his snoring, I was tiptoeing out the front door, down the slick, marble steps, and into the front seat of his car.

When I returned from a trip, I simply parked the car in its original spot, sent the radio dial to its home (a gospel station), and restored the keys to his pants pocket. If another car had filled his parking space in my absence, I parked elsewhere and prayed for my father's forgetfulness. My prayers almost never went unanswered.

One particular night, when my buddy, Ron, and I went to see two girls living in East Baltimore, my usual course was disrupted. As we pulled out of the apartment complex's parking lot, I failed to notice a sign that read "No Left Turn." We were listening to a rap song and doing just as it suggested, "diggin' the scene with our gansta' lean." Our front seats were reclined back nearly onto the back seats. It didn't matter that I couldn't see a thing around me — I was impressing the girls as we were leaving.

The dial on the dashboard clock read 4:00 A.M. I was tired and dreading the rush back into town — I had to make it home, snuggle the "Benz" back into her parking space, fold the keys back into my father's pants pocket, and climb between my own sheets before he awoke.

As I made the illegal left turn, I neither saw nor heard the approaching police car's siren. I noticed not one flash of red light, not one burst of blue. My seat was too far back to catch a glimpse of anything through the rearview mirror, and the radio was blasting too loudly to hear anything else. As soon as I turned, the police car crashed into my dad's '77 Chevy Impala.

The police car had disassembled and was completely wrecked, but because of its hard, steel frame, my dad's car stood strong. Aside from the collapse of the front windshield, driver's side doors, and the bumper hanging somewhere to the side, it remained intact.

The police officer jumped out of his ruined car and ran toward me with a slew of rhetorical questions and one arm waving in fury, all before Ron or I could exit our daze.

"Didn't you see me coming? Didn't you hear my siren? And what are you doing making a left turn here, anyway?"

Before one word of explanation escaped my mouth, he was on the radio calling for backup.

Inside my head, I said a thousand prayers, *Lord, I won't ever take the car again. I won't even get in it with Dad driving.*

90

I won't curse no more, Lord. I won't cut school. I won't fight with my little sister. I won't daydream in church.

Realizing my prayers were useless, I decided I'd better play hurt. Maybe, if my father walked into an emergency room and saw me hanging on to just a thread of life, he might pity me rather than kill me.

The back-up police officers and paramedics arrived, and I pretended to be half-dead. All of a sudden, my eyes were rolled into the back of my head, my feet were tossed inside the dashboard, my body was twisted and pulsating, and my lifeless arm lay contorted in the backseat.

As the paramedics carried me away on a stretcher and hoisted me into the back of the ambulance, I was still hoping for a bit of mercy. A police officer asked for my father's phone number, so he could have him meet us at the hospital. Not three seconds after I recited it, I had a seizure. I convulsed on that gurney like a newly caught fish, screaming, "Somebody help me! I can't breathe!"

The paramedic closest to me bent down and whispered in my ear, "Boy, shut up. Ain't a darn thing wrong with you."

I ignored that. He was messing with my plan.

"Somebody help me, please!"

At the hospital, a team of doctors rushed over to me. "What's the problem?" they asked. But to answer them too clearly wouldn't save me from Dennie Miller. I acted as if I was drifting in and out of consciousness.

"Where does it hurt?" they persisted.

"Everywhere! Ouch! I'm having a seizure! I'm dying!

Somebody! Anybody! Help me!"

By now, the doctors were all well aware of the non life-threatening injuries I proclaimed to have, and began laughing at me. And before I had said anywhere near the number of prayers I needed, my dad came marching down the emergency-room hallway with my uncle at his side.

I heard their voices and pretended I was dead. When they were beside me, I peeked through my half-closed eyelids to see my father's face. I searched for pity, but found none there.

At moments like this, when my father couldn't contain his emotions, he stuttered beyond comprehension. He couldn't capture and drag one word from his mouth right then. All his feelings ran together in a train of broken syllables, "G-g-g-g-got, ah, ah, g-got, g-got, darn, m-mmmum, mack, Macka mmma, ki, ki, kkkk." He sighed, "Phew!" took a breath, and started back up again. "Ki-, ki-, kill, kill, kill, ki-, ki-, kill, kill, kill, kill ya. Got darn, Michael, I'm gonna kill ya!"

The doctors raced to stop him from wrapping his hands around my neck. While he breathed, and before he began another round of stuttering, I interrupted him.

"Dad, Dad, listen to me! I got about a thousand dollars in my jacket at the house. I was saving up to buy a car. Please, take as much money as you need. Fix the car. Take all of it, if you have to. Please, Dad!"

Between his bouts of stuttering, and his gasps for breath, his mind registered what I'd said. At once, his chest settled back into place. The last words he spoke were as clear as water, "Well, I'll see you when you get home."

Once again, I had survived.

High School High Jinks

After I graduated from middle school, I went to Carver Vocational-Technical High School, where my disruptive behavior took a whole new shape. By this point, nearly everyone had given up on me; likewise, I had given up on myself. I didn't want to change my behavior, nor did I think I could change my behavior. So, when I arrived at Carver, my pattern of behavior followed me like toilet paper to a shoe. During ninth grade, I felt a little pressure to fit in with the cool kids, so I ran the halls, cut class, and took on my familiar role as class clown. At the same time, I discovered girls, and my world began to change.

Although I somehow managed to complete ninth grade, I got suspended in the tenth for beating up a random boy for no reason at all. The school's policy stated that if a student was suspended three times in a year, he or she had to be expelled. As was my character, I felt compelled to test the waters. When faced with my second suspension, I was told I couldn't return without a parent. Naturally, I didn't want my parents to find out I was in trouble again, so I devised a plan: I paid a friend's uncle ten dollars to pretend to be my dad. I knew he was an alcoholic, but I didn't think he would come to the school drunk! He stumbled into the principal's office, smelling like Wild Irish Rose and looking like he hadn't slept in a week. He kept dozing off to sleep during the conference and mistakenly calling me, "Marcus." I said to myself, *Michael, what in the world have you gotten yourself into now?* My makeshift parent conference

93

was about to crumble before my eyes.

The principal, Mrs. Deanna, whom the students called Wonder Woman—because of their resemblance—grew suspicious of my so-called Dad. She had enough sense to know my mom was a well-respected Christian woman who wouldn't allow her husband to embarrass her or impede her son's education. Later that afternoon, Wonder Woman called my mom and asked her if my dad had visited the school earlier that day. When my mom told her he had not, she became fed up and expelled me. I was devastated. Graduating from Carver High School was a Miller family tradition. All of my brothers and sisters had graduated from Carver, and I was to be the eighth person to grace its commencement stage.

My expulsion disarmed me. Suddenly, I wasn't my usual unruly self. I was distraught. I begged and pleaded for Principal Wonder Woman's mercy. Could she please give me another chance? I put my pride aside and vowed that I would be on my very best behavior from that point forward, that I would do everything I was supposed to do...anything she asked of me. I promised to not run the hallways, cut class, crack jokes, or be a class clown. My sincerity stung it was so genuine, but I had cried wolf so many times that Wonder Woman didn't believe me. I couldn't persuade her. She could not trust that if given the opportunity to stay at Carver my disruptive behavior would change. She didn't understand what significance Carver held for me—that it gave me something to aspire to, a reason to want to graduate that had nothing to do with me or my future. I couldn't get my family to understand my point, either. They said Carver was just another school. Nobody understood that Carver was my last hope. If I couldn't go to Carver, I had no motive for finishing school.

For many years, I harbored a lot of anger and bitterness toward Carver High School and its principal. My perception of the expulsion was not that I had placed the burden on myself, but that Carver was to blame. Instead of seeing my role in the matter, I embraced anger, bitterness, and hostility. Learning was my new enemy and my Carver High School experience became yet another race I didn't finish.

High School Dropout

I fully understood that my behavior disrupted the educational process and that it was wrong to bring that drunk to school disguised as my father. I knew I was a class clown and that I was wrong for running down the hallways, but now, all I wanted, all I needed was a chance. Somehow, I knew how bad my life would become if I didn't get that chance. I was on a dim path toward delinquency, and being expelled from Carver High School was my breaking point.

I ended up at Walbrook Senior High. Walbrook was the high-school version of the notoriously violent Lemmel Middle. My conduct rose to the occasion—I behaved worse than I ever had. I rolled with the wrong crowd, and I never went to class. I had plenty of opportunities to get into trouble, and I took advantage of each and every one of them.

At the time, the school was being renovated. To accommodate all of its students during the process, Walbrook merged with another high school–Southwestern High–for three years. This merger sparked tensions between the schools and made it difficult for the administration to keep up with all the students. The schools started and ended at different times and because the teachers couldn't keep up with both schools bell schedules, more students cut classes, roamed the halls without passes, got into fights, and left school early.

Within a year, I had been completely discouraged. I had been drained of any motivation to finish school and my aspiration to succeed disappeared. The streets were calling me…and I answered.

I was a typical high-school dropout, spending most of my time trying to find a decent job that didn't require a high-school diploma. There were no decent jobs available. Not unless you didn't mind cleaning toilets. Looking at the other high-school dropouts in my community, I understood why people without an education were looked down upon. Many of them ended up in jail, on street corners selling drugs, or shot and killed. Life as a dropout offered no hope. I didn't know anyone with a high-school diploma who'd made it in Sandtown, much less who'd gone to college.

Are You a Thermostat or a Thermometer?

One of the reasons I dropped out of school was because I could not handle the many pressures it promised. When pressure came my way, I didn't know how to cope. It's important to understand there is a pivotal difference between a thermostat and a thermometer. A thermometer reflects its environment. It simply shows what the temperature is. It doesn't affect anything in its environment. It just registers the rising or falling of the temperature. It exerts no influence on what surrounds it; rather it is influenced by its environment.

A thermostat, though, is different. It measures the temperature and then responds accordingly. If the temperature is too high, a thermostat shuts off the heat. If the temperature is too low, it triggers the heat to turn on. It measures temperature and it does something about it. Just as a thermostat registers its surroundings and changes them when needed, we should not simply rise and fall in response to problems and difficulties in our lives. We should not passively allow harmful situations to happen, feeling as if we have no power.

We must become more like thermostats–motivated by difficulty and adjusting to change. We must believe that something can be done, a solution can be found, and a hurt can be healed.

Advice columnist Ann Landers once said, "If I were asked to give what I consider the single most useful bit of advice for all humanity, it would be this: Expect trouble as an inevitable part of life. When it comes, hold your head high, look it squarely in the eye, and say, 'I will be bigger than you. You cannot defeat me.'" In other words, respond courageously and creatively.

Shun not the Struggle

A great running back in the NFL is judged not by how many yards he runs in a season, but by how many yards he runs after his initial contact with the opposing team. In your race in life race, expect to struggle at times. It is not the struggle that matters. However, it is how you deal with the struggle that makes all the difference. Nothing worthwhile is easy. Frederick Douglass once said, "If there is no struggle, there is no progress." In order to progress in life, we must struggle at times.

The story of the butterfly clearly illustrates the necessity of struggle:

A man stumbled upon a cocoon of a butterfly. A small opening appeared. He sat down beside it and watched its birth for several hours. The fragile insect pushed its nearly transparent wings against the cocoon's walls. The butterfly struggled to force its body through that extremely small hole with much pain. For a long while it seemed to stop making any progress. It appeared as if it had gone as far as it could, and that it could go no farther.

So the man—naïve—decided to help the butterfly. He took a pair of scissors and snipped off the remaining bit of the cocoon. The butterfly then emerged easily—it seemed to slide from its cage like water off glass—but it had a swollen body and small, shriveled wings. The man continued to observe the butterfly. He expected, at any moment, for the wings to enlarge and the body to contract. Neither happened! In fact, the butterfly spent the rest of its short life crawling around with a bloated body and wrinkled wings. It was never able to fly. The man had acted with well-intentioned kindness, but didn't foresee the consequences of his actions. The restricting cocoon and the struggle required to get through the tiny opening, were nature's way of forcing fluid from the butterfly's body. In this way, it would've achieved its freedom from the cocoon.

Sometimes struggles are precisely what we need. If we were to go through life without any obstacles, we would be crippled at the first sign of pain. We would not be as strong as we could've been, and we could never fly.

The next time you're faced with an obstacle, a challenge or a problem, remember the butterfly. Struggle a bit. Bend and straighten your weak wings against the wall of your cocoon. Rest. Begin again, and then fly! Stay focused on the finish line. And while you are on your way, *SHUN NOT THE STRUGGLE!...* *It's God's gift!*

Chapter 5

No Free Rides:

Life as a High School Dropout

"Every time I come in the kitchen, you in the kitchen. In the godd@mn refrigerator. Eatin' up all the food. All the chitlins. All the pig's feet. All the collard greens. All the hog maws. I wanna eat them chitlins. I like pig's feet! — I want you to get you're a_ _ up today, go out and look for a job! The word today is — job. J-o-b! You hear me?"

—Mr. Jones, Friday

free ride - *noun. slang.* something that can be acquired without the usual effort or cost.

My father made it clear that there were no free rides in his household. Anything I wanted, I had to work hard for it. Plain and simple.

He would say, "Boy, if you are not in school, you will get a job and work. And if you don't, you will git da hell out of here!"

When I first dropped out of school at the age of sixteen, I thought I was on top of the world. I had the mentality of a superstar, and I was certain I was special. I felt safe on the streets, confident that my street-smarts would enable me to handle any situation that might arise.

My dad required the grown children living in his house to pay twenty dollars a week to cover rent, food, utilities, and telephone expenses. Instead of paying the money, I griped about all the money I thought he was trying to make. I didn't realize he was trying to instill accountability, responsibility, and the art of living on a budget within us. By requiring us to pay bills that we would eventually have to pay on our own, my father was giving us a taste of what adult life would be like once we finally did leave home.

Though twenty dollars is only a small percentage of the cost of running a household, I thought it was too much money, so I decided to take my dad's advice to those who wouldn't abide by his rules: Move out. "If ya don't like it, you can ge-ge-ge-ge-get out!" he'd say. "Shoot, I pa-pa-pay da bills around dis here house. If you don't like my rules, g-g-g-go — and, ah, rah, get your own place a-a-and ah, ah, m-m-make, make [pause] make your own damn rules."

So that's what I did. I was eighteen years old and, at least in my own eyes, officially a man. I moved out of my parent's house with an income that was hardly stable.

I found an inexpensive apartment for two-hundred-eighty dollars a month. Although it was two-hundred dollars more than I was used to paying, I thought I could afford it. The only things I moved into my new apartment were my clothes and a clean set of sheets. I didn't even have a bed. Because I couldn't afford a mattress I had to improvise, so I put my clothes under the sheets and slept on them. Food was another problem. I quickly realized my parents weren't cooking for me anymore and that I didn't know how to cook, so I ordered pizza and Chinese food every day of the week.

With my newly acquired apartment came newly acquired bills, and with those new bills, my funds promptly ran low. After paying the bills–not including the rent itself–I had little or no money left over to eat. I felt homeless in my new home because I was hungry all the time. But I couldn't bring myself to move back home. My image was more important than eating or keeping warm. Meanwhile, my money continued to wane. I was trying to be "Mr. Big Shot" and make it on my own. By this time, I was filled with too much pride to ask for any type of assistance from anyone. I thought, *I'm grown now. I gotta find my own way.* So, I took the now-and-later approach to survival. I would eat a meal now and save the leftovers for later. I'd preserve food in the refrigerator to eat throughout the week until it was empty again. Or I'd stop by my parents' house to say hello and sneak in a free meal. I would grab a few extra pieces of chicken and some biscuits at dinner, and then I was ready to go home. That was my weekly routine, especially on Sundays.

Meanwhile, my house was void of furniture and life. Sometimes, the only edible items in my refrigerator were lard and water. No one knew about my poverty. I had too much pride. I pretended that my apartment was fully furnished and that I had my finances under control. During the second month, I finally managed to buy a bed by postponing payment on my rent. By the third month, I bought a living room set and a television. I figured that my apartment was presentable enough to invite my girlfriend, Nikki, over to see how I was living. In the meantime, rent was still due. I hadn't paid rent since I'd started living there and that had been three months ago, and the unpaid bills were piling up.

I purposely avoided paying my bills so I could furnish my apartment and present it to guests. My goal was to build a cozy ambience. My best friend Ron, the same friend who was with me when the police officer crashed into my dad's car, soon moved in with me. His girlfriend's frequent visits turned into frequent sleepovers. She ended up moving in. I was trying to help my buddy Ron and his girlfriend, and I barely had the means to take care of myself.

Not surprisingly, I got evicted. One morning, after living in my first apartment for just four months, I received an unexpected visit from the rent-court constable, accompanied by the maintenance men who came to set my belongings outside. He knocked on the door and asked me if I could pay the past due rent to avoid eviction for nonpayment. I told him that I could go and get it. He shook his head and said, "No, sir, we don't have time for that. If you can't give the property manager the total balance due immediately, we're going to have to evict you from this apartment."

My pride disintegrated. Frantic and desperate, I begged and pleaded, "Sir, please, I can go get the money right now. You see, I planned on paying it, but I never had a chance to make it to the rental office. I was going to make the payment the other day, but the rental office was closed."

Yeah, right! The rental office was right next door to my apartment. He knew I was lying and continued to shake his head 'No'. Desperate, I continued my already failing negotiations, "As a matter of fact, now that I think about it, I paid the rent the other day." My story was too inconsistent and unbelievable, and I knew he knew I was telling a flat-out lie. It was too late. The maintenance men whizzed past me, scooped up all of my belongings, and set them out on the street. I felt humiliated with everything I owned sitting on the curb, and thoroughly ashamed that I had let my financial responsibilities get out of control. Even the girl next door who'd had a crush on me witnessed my eviction. Figuring I had nothing to lose, I asked her for her phone number.

"Oh, no!" she replied emphatically, "You must be trippin'! I don't want a man who's broke and can't pay his bills!"

So there I was on the curb with my cozy apartment furniture. My apartment was in a rural neighborhood, so I had to walk about a mile to use the pay phone to call my dad to come and get me. By the time I walked back to my belongings, just about everything was gone except for my pillow. I couldn't believe people would come by and steal my belongings. By then, I was like a dog on a fire hydrant —pissed off!

Being on my own meant I had to accept my responsibilities. After this episode, I realized I wasn't as ready for those responsibilities as I thought. I thought I was a man because I was living on my own, but I still had the mentality of a boy. I failed to realize that being a man meant not only *having* responsibilities, but also *taking care* of them. Just because I was legally old enough to live on my own, didn't mean I was mature enough to do so.

More importantly, I realized as I sat on the curb with my few remaining possessions, while the rest of my belongings were scattered across the city, that my possessions didn't make me a man. I realized that spending the past four months trying to furnish an apartment rather than paying its bills was a poor choice. My freedom, too, had been stolen. The irony was that I had stolen it from myself by being irresponsible.

Life is all about choices, and my choices had taken me right back to where I'd started, to the place I had tried so desperately to escape from — the place I had called home for the last eighteen years of my life. I went back to Riggs Avenue.

How Ya' Living?

I must admit that I was one who felt I didn't deserve to live at all. After I dropped out of school, I hung out on the streets every day, doing nothing to better myself. I tried to find various jobs, but nothing stuck. I was also dealing with a secret I had never confessed to anyone, not even to God, Himself. I could barely read. And although God knew my shameful secret, I didn't talk to Him about it. I tried to suppress it into the darkness of my soul, thinking that one day it wouldn't matter. But it only haunted me. All of the days in school spent being a class clown, cutting class, skipping school, and not reading regularly had caught up with me and threatened to defeat me.

Because of my illiteracy, I couldn't even fill out a job application. When asked my sex on an application, I would write "Every day."

Are You Living or Just Alive?

When I first dropped out of high school, I was *alive* but I wasn't *living*. And there is a fundamental difference between being *alive* and *living* (and between *dying* and being *dead*, for that matter). Living is doing more than what needs to be done, and being alive is doing just enough to get by. Most people, it seems, do just enough to keep themselves *alive*, but not enough to *live*. They don't start living until they receive some drastic wake-up call. Those who don't need such a call experience many more happy years than the average person.

Often, it's not what somebody else is doing to us, rather, it's what we're doing to ourselves that causes our depression. It saddens me to know so many African-American teenagers, especially boys, are addicted to marijuana and other drugs and involved with gang violence. I can definitely relate to that. Unfortunately, these boys think, just as I did, that manhood is not about building a future, but about how much time they can do in jail. Many young people, including so-called men over eighteen, think manhood is about how many babies they can make without raising them. Many of them think real men call their women b_tches, whores, sluts, and tricks. Well, silly rabbit, tricks are for kids! Because if you call a woman a b_tch, which is a female dog, and you were born from the womb of a woman, then what does that make you? The answer: a puppy. Better yet, that would make you a "Son-of-a b_tch."

Conversely, many women declare, "All men are dogs."

But the Bible tells us that man was created in the image of God. How can women state that all men are dogs when at the same time it's declared that man was created in the image of God? By doing so, you're not just rejecting men, you are subconsciously rejecting God. Likewise, if you believe that all men are dogs and continue to date this type of man, then that makes you just what he's calling you—a b_tch—because you are subconsciously being the female dog he proclaims you to be. Sisters, do not continue to buy music by men who insult and degrade women. Thus, these so-called men are getting *rich* by calling you a *b_tch.*

So don't "eat" anything that's thrown your way, nor should you "sleep" with any other dog that's just laying "in the alley." It would be more flattering to know who you are, not what you can sexually do for a person or what your physical attributes are. Remember what I said earlier: show them your MIND, not your BEHIND!

Many women get upset when their men (or male consumers) leave them for another woman because of her physical attributes. The question becomes, what did you "advertise" to him? What did you get him to "buy" into? Did you come with a high price tag attached to you, or did he "buy" you on sale? Did you allow yourself to be put on "lay-away?"

Unfortunately, many of us are suffering from what I call "unconscious, low self-esteem." Although we may not be conscious of this low self-esteem, we are subconsciously exhibiting its symptoms. Because we think poorly of ourselves, we sit back and wait for the pleasures of life to fall into our laps. To rise above this mentality takes *faith* and *fortitude*. It takes grit and grace. It takes *Divine* help and *human* determination.

Are You Living for the Weekend?

Many people are more concerned with finding thrills than fulfilling their purpose in life. The Reverend Al Sharpton once said, "Anytime you just live from thrill to thrill, you have reduced yourself from a child of God to some freak of the Devil." Now all the Devil has to do is thrill you, and you're ready for the next thrill. The musical group, Farrar, once wrote a song entitled, "We're living for the weekend." But how can you live for the weekend, when most of the week is not the weekend? Do you think five days out of every week are nothing? That most of your life is an irrelevant waste of time? If you've been reduced to a freak of the Devil, whatever and whoever *thrills* you *controls* you.

And it isn't just thrill-seekers who allow themselves to be controlled. I always wanted to control myself, but with my lack of education, I was being controlled by the system. I was controlled by where I lived. When I was incarcerated as a juvenile, I was told by what time I was allowed to eat, sleep, and watch TV. I've heard people say things like, "They're trying to move Black people to the suburbs." If you're on welfare, others can dictate where you live. But if you take charge of your own life, the system can't dictate where you live.

Above all, I've learned a lesson that I will never forget: In life, there are no free rides. You must develop a strong work ethic.

The Breaking Point

My childhood was marked by my father's absence. Our family's livelihood depended on him, and his determination to sustain us pushed him to work constantly. It was this very determination which prevented him from spending quality time with me or any of his children. For this reason, I yearned for his retirement. I viewed his work schedule as an impossible obstacle — as long as my father worked, I would never truly know him. With his retirement, I could begin to learn his ways, his thoughts, and his dreams. I could begin to feel like his son.

With just a year of work to go, I could hardly contain my excitement. Finally we would converse. We would laugh until our stomachs ached. We would hang out and share meals. We would make up for a lifetime of emptiness. In twelve months, I would say "Daddy" and truly understand what it meant to be loved by the man of that name.

Three months into my father's final year of work, with just nine months before the forging of our new relationship, he succumbed to kidney failure. I lost him just prior to his retirement, and he'd never known the feeling of a workless day. Suddenly, this honorable man, well-respected in our home and community, was taken. A cold day in March 1996 left me distraught and with the distinct feeling that I would travel life's difficult journey alone.

A few months after my father's death, I was the same man — unemployed and uneducated, yet his physical absence complicated things further, and I was near desperation. At twenty-five, I was tired. My life had been a series of disappointments and misfortunes. I could barely see myself through, let alone view life optimistically. My pitfalls had overwhelmed me, and in a single, bleak moment I felt no hope. I wanted to banish all the pain and sorrow; I wanted to wash away the unbearable hurt over my father's death. I could not conceptualize tomorrow.

I asked myself, *Why keep running just to come in last place, anyway? Why pretend that things are going to get better? Why should I even try?* With nothing left to hold onto, I gave up. Out of the darkness and desolation of my soul, I cried out for death to comfort me. I decided to commit suicide and put an end to it all.

I called a hospital inquiring about the number of pills necessary to induce suicide. Thinking she was answering a hypothetical question, the nurse on the other end asked, "How much has the person taken? And what kind of medication is it?"

I answered, "A small half bottle of Tylenol."

The woman, either unaware or unconcerned that I was asking for myself, told me, "If a person takes at least a bottle, I suggest you take them to the emergency room."

Determined to end my pain forever, I took two large bottles of extra-strength Tylenol. It was around 11:00 P.M. on a summer night. After ingesting the pills, I drove away from downtown Baltimore with no destination in mind. After an hour, I started to feel very dizzy and sick to my stomach. I pulled the car into a high-school parking lot, thinking I could recuperate from the nausea. I don't remember much after that. My only memory is falling down in the school's football field.

Somehow, I'd walked to the field's center and collapsed. I laid there, in the darkness, for an hour or more.

Sometime before I'd submitted completely to the pills, a friend of mine, Tim, noticed my parked car. Tim, a minister, didn't usually hang around the heart of the ghetto, but for some reason, he was there. After searching the neighborhood extensively, he was compelled to walk through the football field. Pitch black, the field offered no light by which to see, but Tim, sightless, trekked through it. Eventually, he noticed that I was collapsed in the middle of the dark football field.

I vaguely remember Tim's voice in my ear saying, "Mike, Mike, hang in there, buddy." I also remember him making an earnest petition and crying out to God — "Father, I stretch out my hands to thee. There is no other help that I know!" Ironically, these were the same words my mother used when she was fed up and didn't know what else to do with me. Immediately following Tim's plea, I passed out. I fell into a deep sleep that promised to rescue me from all of the pain. I just knew peace was coming, that I was through with my sorrow forever.

And then, suddenly, I was in an emergency room with tubes shoved down my throat and a hospital staff working frantically to pump from me as many pills as they could. Despite the choking sensation inspired by the tubes, I cursed and hollered. The gagging reflex didn't prevent me from expressing the anger over my rescue — I let the doctors and nurses know they weren't saving a grateful man. Once the staff had done all they could, they gave me some thick syrup to soak up the remainder of the medicine in my system. This syrup was the worst thing I'd ever tasted. It was thick and black, with a chalky taste, but I was forced to tolerate it. I wanted so much to go back to sleep, this time forever, but no one would allow my departure.

I was anxious to leave the hospital to try again, because my plan had been mysteriously thwarted, and this time I was going to try the surest way out.

"No, Mr. Miller. You can't leave here right now. We have to make sure that you're safe," one of the doctors said.

"Uh no the hell y'all won't!" I replied. "I'm getting the hell up out of here! You can't tell me what to do. I'm a grown man! You must be out of your d@mn mind, doc!" I didn't care about my safety. I wanted to be free of my pain.

I tried to leave the hospital, but the doctors screamed out, "Security!" The next thing I knew, I was upstairs in the Cuckoo for Coco Puffs ward.

Didn't they get the picture? Couldn't they see I was tired of running my race? It didn't matter to me then that it was only by the Grace of God that I'd survived the suicide attempt. I just wanted to be free of my pain. I wanted to forfeit the race. Within the doors of the psychiatric ward, my spirit died. I fell down — way down — without a single thought of getting back up again.

Part 2

.....But We Get Up!

"Every morning in Africa, a gazelle wakes up.
It knows it must outrun the fastest lion or it will
be killed. Every morning in Africa, a lion
wakes up. It knows it must run faster than the
slowest gazelle, or it will starve. It doesn't matter whether you're a lion or a gazelle-when the
sun comes up, you'd better be running!"

—Dr. Calvin Mackie

Chapter 6

Get Back Up Again!:

Looking Back to Move Forward

"Proverbs 24:16 says: *A just man falls seven times, but rises back up again.* Now what makes him just? Most of us in the church would call him wicked if he falls seven times. So what makes him just from the Bible's standpoint? It's that he has enough sense to rise back up. And not only get back up, but get back in line."

—Donnie McClurkin

to get up - *verb.* to rise to ones feet from a fall.

As weak and exhausted as I was, I summoned the courage to get back in the race. Over time, my anklebones strengthened, my legs fortified, and my heart filled with life. For the first time in twenty-five years, I stood on my own two feet. Sure, I was unsteady at first, but hope rushed and grabbed me by one arm, faith took me by the other, and perseverance said, "Follow me." I put one foot forward and said, "This step is for the baggage I've been carrying — all the hurt, pain, anguish, guilt, and turmoil I've suffered." I took a second step, and said, "This is for all the anger and animosity I've carried against everyone, including God." The third step felt best because it represented my failure as a father. "This," I said "is for the parent I've never been." "I'm alive," I said, "Now it's time to live."

In Search of My Son

At this point, I realized I needed to be a real man and become a father to my son. All the pain, misery, worries, doubts, setbacks, and obstacles I'd faced (and would continue to face) were nothing more than speed bumps devised to slow me down long enough to teach me some lessons. Once I'd crossed them, and heeded their message, I'd accelerate again toward my ultimate destination.

I knew God had a purpose for my life once I'd miraculously survived my suicide attempt. So, I asked Him for a chance to right my wrongs. I promised God, if granted just one opportunity, I would do everything humanly possible to straighten my crooked path. With that covenant, God and I worked together to transform my life. Before I could consider moving very far forward, though, I had to take an anguished look into my past. I had to retrace my footsteps and find my lost sheep — my son.

The word *Sankofa*, which comes from the Akan people of Ghana, West Africa, is derived from the words *san* (return), *ko* (go), and *fa* ("look," "seek," and "take," respectively). Translated, it means, "to move forward, one must return to the past." The concept is often symbolized by a bird flying forward with its head turned backward.

Sankofa helped me recognize the importance of self-evaluation and resolving past hurts to determine my future. At age twenty-five, I realized it was time to retrace my footsteps and mend the relationship with my son. Finding him would be no easy task since Dévon and his mother had been missing from my life for nearly six years. Though I pretended not to have a conscience, I did. I'd simply chosen to ignore it. While in high school, I had been told by Candy's foster sister that Candy had lost custody of all of her children as a result of her drug abuse, but I never paid it much attention.

Surprisingly, after all those years of neglect, I actually found him. After seeking out his mother's family and calling a few government agencies, I found out my son was in the custody of the Department of Social Services. But, I had to put up a hell of a fight before I could see him.

Man on a Mission

When I went to the Department of Social Services, I was informed that my parental rights had been terminated.

"How can that be?" I asked.

"Your son is about to be adopted by his foster parents. I guess it's too late to be a father now, Mr. Miller."

I knew I couldn't take no for an answer. Something crazy had to be done. Just like everything else in life, "All things are possible for those who believe." Even if no one had done it before, I was going to take care of my son. I asked the social worker, "Ma'am, is it possible for me to get my parental rights back?"

She replied, "Well, Mr. Miller, at this stage, it's very difficult for that to happen."

"But is it possible?" I persisted.

"Why are you trying to interrupt something that's going along just fine?" she asked.

My response was, "Because I'm on a mission!"

When someone's parental rights have been terminated, it's usually definitive. Most parents give up and stop fighting the system. It's a long, hard, tedious battle. But I was on a mission. All I wanted to know was if it was possible. That's it.

The social worker said sarcastically, "Mr. Miller, it will take a miracle."

I smiled and said, "That's all I need to know!"

"But we're about to go through the final stages of the adoption," she reminded me. She continued to try to break my persistent spirit by telling me about all the petitions I'd have to file. Subsequently, I would have to show just cause for why I hadn't been in the picture until now. Then the judge would have to award me custody if he felt that I had grounds for reinstating my parental rights.

"Mr. Miller, do you have an attorney?" she asked.

"No," I replied. "My mother told me that God is a lawyer in the court room. I'll just represent myself. I've got Jesus, and that's enough!"

The social worker continued her sarcastic remarks and questions, all with the intent of deterring my destination, "Do you have a job and a home in your name that would provide suitable living conditions for a child? You will have to meet the requirements of the home inspector. How are you providing for yourself? Do you know how to care for a child? What is your show-cause reason why your rights should be reinstated? Where were you the last six to eight years of his life? Right now, Mr. Miller, it's you against the Department of Social Services, because we're not recommending that your rights be reinstated. I just don't see it happening. Now, what is your response to that?"

Got Faith!

I was silent. I didn't have a response to give to her, because I couldn't fulfill any of the qualifications which she listed.

"Yeah, that's what I thought," she replied. Then her voice got louder and she said, "You're just a typical dead-beat dad with an excuse. So, Mr. Miller, what do you have, then? You don't have a home. You don't have a lawyer. You don't have a show-cause reason for the judge to reinstate your parental rights. You can't even tell me where you've been for the last six to eight years of your son's life. Well, it's too late now. So, what do you have?"

I looked her straight in the eyes, as I yelled out, loud and clear, "Faith!"

Everything became silent. She was stunned by my humble yet arrogant response. Instantly, she backed away from me and sat down.

I continued to look deeply into her eyes to let her know that I was going to fight. Even if it meant going against the entire Department of Social Services, even if it meant putting my life on the line, even if it meant losing everything, I was going to fight. I was on a mission! I then left her office without another word spoken.

Although I had faith, I needed God to show up right away and give me directions. Things weren't looking very good for me, but for some strange reason, my faith remained steady. In others words, I lost hope, but my faith remained. The difference between the two is profound. Hope is desire accompanied by possibility and faith is trust accompanied by certainty. And belief or faith is the conduit through which God does the impossible.

Order My Steps

I knew my mission as a father was to reclaim that which I'd lost — my son. And I was not going to stop until my mission was complete. Even though the Department of Social Services had cast me out, I would continue to walk by faith and not by sight. I found great comfort and inspiration in knowing that the Bible declares, *"The steps of a good man are ordered by God, and he delights in his way. Though he falls, he shall not be utterly cast down."* –Psalms 37: 23–24.

Regardless of everything the social worker said, I had received the orders to fulfill my mission. And what a lonely mission it was. I went back and forth to court, trying to file the petition to regain my parental rights. If it wasn't one thing, it was another. Either the weather caused the courts to close down or one of the other attorneys didn't show up. Then there were postponements due to the judge's crowded docket, thus postponing the case until further notice. It was always something. I went back and forth to the petition hearing nine different times before the case was finally heard.

I didn't need a lawyer. Just like my mom, I walked in with favor and faith, and I represented myself.

All Things Are Possible!

Dr. Benjamin Elijah Mays once gave the charge to the Morehouse College graduating class of 1961 and said, "May you forever stand for something noble and high. Let no man dismiss you with a wave of the hand or a shrug of the shoulder." I tried to uphold those words. I was adamant that I would not let anyone "dismiss me with a wave of the hand or a shrug of the shoulder." I was determined to be heard.

The Department of Social Services' attorney and my son's attorney were representing the best interest of the child; they were both contesting against me. Yet, I stood resolute. After a year of grueling battles, the judge awarded my parental rights on the basis of a technicality. Neither my numerous appearances before him nor my many drastic changes in lifestyle won his favor, rather the fact that I had not been legally notified of the termination of my parental rights secured the reclamation of my fatherhood.

It's amazing how everything works together for those who believe. My mission was not over just yet — I still had to battle to get custody of my son — but in the meantime, I had visitation rights, and this decision put a screeching halt to the adoption proceedings. Although the Department of Social Services wanted my son to be adopted by the family he was living with, as long as I met the necessary requirements, they had to work out a plan for reunification with me.

Initially, I was only permitted to see Dévon for the minimum one-hour visitation the law allowed. This was partly because I gave the social workers such a headache every chance I got. We constantly disagreed about the best interests of my son. They just wanted to go forward with the adoption and I wouldn't allow it. I was determined to gain custody of Dévon. Many times, things got so chaotic between us that our telephone conversations ended in heated arguments.

I refused to let them dismiss me as a typical dead-beat dad. I wanted to make sure they did their job. One of the things I've learned from dealing with the system is that if you allow them to run over you, they will. Some social workers genuinely have the children's best interests at heart, but many seem to be lazy or overburdened with too many cases to meet success.

The court system was ardently opposed to letting a young man who hadn't been in the picture for a while raise his son. In fact, the court records show that I went to court forty-three times in reference to my son. Although they made me jump through all kinds of hoops to get custody of Dévon, I didn't falter. So fathers, it's possible to win a parental rights' case. You just have to be devoted, diligent, and extremely determined.

It's Never Too Late

Some people want to put restrictions on themselves according to their lack of talent, intelligence, or experience.

Others worry about their age. One person can always make a difference, regardless of his or her circumstances or situation. As the old adage goes, "age aint nothing but a number." So, you're never too old — or too young — to finish what you've started. I remember once asking a group of nontraditional college students what they planned to do after they graduated. One student said, "Well, Mr. Miller, I would love to go to medical school for eight years and become a doctor, but I'll be forty-two years old by the time I finish medical school."

My response was, "It doesn't really matter. In eight years, you're gonna be forty-two years old anyway. You might as well be forty-two years old....And be a Doctor!

You must understand that change is inevitable, but growth is optional. Change will always come, but you've got to make the choice to grow.

Are you My Daddy?

The time finally came for me to visit my son. We started out with one-hour visitations, with the social worker listening in on our conversations. Social Services thought this arrangement would discourage me from visiting him, but it didn't. I'll never forget seeing him for the first time since he was an infant. As he walked toward me, he looked like an exact replica of me as a child. He asked me, "Are you my daddy?" And I responded with, "Yes, son, I'm your daddy."

I was trying really hard not to cry, but I began to break. I couldn't help but to release the emotion I had been holding back for so long. As we drew closer to each other in what would be a long embrace, my heart began to beat really fast. Tears began to pour down his face and he looked at me fearfully. It seemed as if he was afraid, afraid of being attached to his parents again and of being left alone again. After all, he had been moving from one foster home to the next. And, at that time, I was a stranger to him.

I kept reassuring him that everything was okay. As we hugged each other during this emotional moment, I began to feel what he was going through. He squeezed me tightly, as if he was desperately in need of a father to hug, to hold, and to cherish. It felt like a hug that had been backed up for many years. I wasn't used to hugging my parents, my friends, my brothers or my sisters. I wasn't used to that kind of love and affection. Hugging my son for the first time felt so good! It felt warm; it felt charming; it felt sincere; it felt genuine; and it made me feel needed as a father.

Escaping with Excuses

While we embraced each other, I whispered in my son's ear something I should have said a long time before. I said to him, with emotion, "I'm sorry. I'm so very sorry, Dévon. It wasn't my fault."

All he could do was cry his heart out, "Daddy, where were you?" He kept asking questions I was not prepared to answer, "Daddy, where were you when they came to get me? What took you so long to come see me? Why weren't you there when I needed a father?"

I began to make up what I thought were legitimate excuses

for my absence. I told him I didn't know where he and his mom were when they moved. However, that wasn't what my eight-year-old son wanted or needed to hear. The truth was, if I had wanted to, I could have found him.

Not once during the conversation did I take the blame for what had happened. Not once did I take the blame for my faults. Not once did I admit to my eight-year-old son that I had partly caused the pain he was feeling or explain why I hadn't been there to catch him when he was falling. I didn't have any answers, only excuses. He didn't want to hear excuses. He wanted the truth so that true healing could begin.

We can't help or heal with lies. Dévon wanted to stop feeling the pain of not having his parents there when he needed them. He wanted the same thing that all other kids want: He wanted to call someone 'Mama' or 'Daddy', regardless of what his mother had done. What about Daddy? It didn't matter that they had moved. The years my son spent crying himself to sleep were nobody's fault but mine.

Why, Daddy? Why?

While I stood there, as Dévon cried, I began to realize he was feeling much like I did when I was his age. The context was different, but the emotion was the same. My father lived with me, but he stayed busy most of the time and was unable to give me his earnest attention. Now Dévon cried out for attention just as I once had, "Why, Daddy? Why?"

When Dévon asked, "Daddy, where were you?" or "Why, Daddy? Why?" I threw a barrage of excuses in my son's face

127

that were intended to make him feel sorry for me. But Dévon, even as a child, could cut through all that nonsense. For every excuse I made, Dévon came back with a corresponding challenge.

I said to him, "I didn't know where you were. Your mother had moved and it was hard to find you."

And Dévon responded, "But why, Daddy? Why couldn't you find me?"

When I said, "I never had a father figure to teach me how to be a father," he responded with his continued tears and the repeated question of, "But why, Daddy? Why?" He wasn't fooled by my attempts to blame others for my failures.

Seeking for the Solutions

As he walked away, I stood there, feeling puzzled. Things had started off okay, with tears of joy, but had ended with tears of pain and many unanswered questions. I left the building trying to figure out what had happened. I found myself upset, angry, and filled with rage. But with whom? God? While I didn't curse at Him this time, I felt betrayed by God. I felt as if He had turned His back on me. What ever happened to "I will never leave you, nor forsake you?" I felt like God had set me up for failure, to be rejected by my own son. I was obedient to His great commission to go back and reclaim my son, only to find myself rejected. There I was, in the middle of downtown fussing with God, saying, "You set me up."

People were walking by me and saying, "He must be crazy!"

I began to get discouraged. Voices were going through my

head, saying, "Michael, you might as well give up. You can't fix a relationship that has already been broken. It's too late!"

The Man in the Mirror

The race of life is tough. You either get distracted or discouraged. You begin to doubt what you're doing and to question yourself. You stumble and get knocked down, but winners get back up and keep going. Just as Aaliyah suggested, we must dust ourselves off and try again. And that's exactly what I did.

I walked through the streets of downtown Baltimore trying to find a solution to this madness. Everyone else was at fault except Michael. As I was walking along, I heard the lyrics to a Michael Jackson song on the radio, "I'm talking 'bout the Man in the Mirror/ I'm asking him to change his ways/ And no message could have been any clearer/ If you wanna make the world a better place/ take a look at yourself and make that change!"

The Apology and the Promise

As I listened, it occurred to me that I had to look at myself and admit my own wrongdoings. Therefore, I decided to heed the lyrics of the song, take a look at myself, and make that change! During the next visit, a week later, I made sure my approach was much different. As soon as I walked into the visitation room, I told him very genuinely and affectionately, "Son, I understand what you're going through. It wasn't your fault. It was mine. I'm very sorry you had to go through what you went through alone. I'm sorry I wasn't there to hug and kiss you every night and tell you that Daddy loves you. I apologize

129

for making partying and the streets a priority over my own son. If I could turn back the hands of time, son, I would, but I can't. Starting right now, I promise to always be there when you need me. But most of all, I will love you unconditionally, Dévon."

We cried together. All I could do was cry. That thug mentality I thought I had went right out the window. I had finally reclaimed one of the most precious jewels in my life, my son. I had retraced and found my lost sheep. I had been given a second chance to right my wrongs.

That experience has taught me a valuable lesson: Honest and sincere apologies are the key to healing the pains of the past. I started doing what psychologists call introspection or self-examination to try to find out where I had gone wrong. Self-examination is difficult for many of us because it compels us to do a critical analysis of *ourselves*, rather than of other people.

In order to acknowledge my faults, I had to start with the basics like apologizing and admitting my own faults and failures, rather than making excuses for my behavior. In fact, the first step in any type of rehabilitation begins with either one of the Three "A"s: You must Accept, Acknowledge, or Admit that there is a problem. When you accept, acknowledge, or admit you are partly to blame for your problems, you are on your way to solving them. Many people spend their entire lives playing the blame game, convinced they are right all the time, rather than acknowledging the other person's feelings and views.

To stop playing the blame game, I had to acknowledge what I had done wrong, accept what I had lacked as a child, and admit that change had to start with me. As I mentioned before,

I had never witnessed anyone in my community saying, "I was wrong," "I apologize," or, "I'm sorry." But nevertheless, I decided that it was now time for me to face up to my responsibilities and stop making excuses.

No More Excuses

Even though I had never imagined that I would have to work so hard to win back my son, it was time that I corrected my faults by standing up and being a man...a real man. All I had ever given my son was excuses. An old proverb says, "Excuses are like crutches; they're for the lame and the weak." If you continue to make excuses to your child, or for your condition, your life, or for neglecting your responsibilities, then you are lame, weak, or both. It's a harsh statement, but it's true.

George Washington Carver once stated, "Ninety-nine percent of failures come from people who have the habit of making excuses." So many times, we have indoctrinated ourselves to blow the balloons for our own pity parties. We pack our luggage to go on guilt trips. We say it's "The man" who's holding us down, when, in all reality, we're holding *ourselves* down. Many of us believe that if circumstances were different, we would be in a different predicament. Even if that's true, excuses are the language of failure. Blaming others means you are not taking responsibility and ownership of your mistakes in your life. This denial of ownership leads to a victim mentality and allows important opportunities to pass you by. It's easy to point the finger at everyone else's wrongdoings, but not our own. Remember, when you point a single finger at someone else, three fingers are literally pointing back at you.

Throughout my race in life, I would always blame others for my failures. I kept saying to my son, "I didn't know where you were! My father was never there to teach me how to be a father. I come from a community where I didn't see positive role models of fathers."

The truth is I failed to look for my son and had consciously decided not to seek him out. I also used my background as an excuse for my failures. This was my crutch. Now let's be real. Racism is not responsible for African-Americans killing each other—*we are!* Growing up without a father in the house is not the reason you're a deadbeat dad–*you are!* Your boyfriend or girlfriend is not getting on your nerves so badly that you have to go behind their back and cheat on them–*you want to!* You're not getting bad job reviews because your boss doesn't like you– *you're lazy!* You didn't get a failing grade in class because your teacher had something against you–you didn't do your work! Nobody else is responsible for your failure—*it's you; it's you; it's you; it's you!*

We Fall Down, But We Get Up!

On your way to reaching your destination, you're going to stumble and take a few falls. When that happens, you've got to have the fervor and fortitude to get back up again, dust yourself off, and get going.

I've learned that as long as you lie down and remain stretched out, *passive* and *inactive*, you'll always make excuses for your failures. And as long as you keep talking about how bad things are, you'll never go anywhere, and you'll never do anything.

Even if you are down, you don't have to stay there and adjust. If I were to step in front of you and knock you off your feet, that's on *me*. But if you're still lying there the following week, that's on *you*. Though you may not be responsible for being down, you're still responsible for getting back up again. If you should ever fall down, make sure you fall on your back, because if you can look up, you can get up!

Yes, life is hard. Yes, life may tear you down and knock you down. In fact, life may knock you to your knees. But as I've found out, that's a good praying position!

Your condition is not your conclusion. Your current status does not dictate where you can go. It doesn't matter what you've been through, you can always fix what has been broken. Its not our fault how we started life, but it is our responsibility how we finish. No matter how many times you've fallen before, GET BACK UP, AGAIN!

Stop living in the past and put the past where it should be–behind you. It was only meant to propel you into the promise of your future. Your past should be a reference, not a residence. We can become so overwhelmed by failures and mistakes that we just stop running, letting past failures paralyze present opportunities.

So, if you want things to get better in your life, you have to rise and stand up to the situation! You have to rise above your obstacles so you can say, "I can be knocked down, but I will not be knocked out."

Choosing to lie down will *sap* your strength, but choosing

to stand up will *give* you strength. Lying down *takes* your courage, but standing up *gives* you courage. Lying down, you'll *wear* other people out, but standing up, you'll just *wear out*! So stop lying down and waiting around for somebody to do something for you. Take charge of your life and *Get back up again!*

Chapter 7
Begin with the End in Mind:
The Art of the Start

"The journey of a thousand miles begins with a single step."

—Lao Tzu

"You don't have to be great to get started, but you have to get started to be great."

—Les Brown

begin - *verb.* to take the first step in doing; to start.
end - *noun.* something toward which one strives; a goal.
mind - *noun.* focus of thought; attention.

Everything is possible once the runners have settled into the starting blocks for the race. Within a microsecond of the starter judge announcing, "Runners, take your mark! . . . get set! . . ." the runners brace themselves to burst out of the blocks. When the starter's pistol cracks, the sprinters vault forward, expecting a win. But before they reach the finish line, they may fall, tear a muscle, or simply lose focus. Some may not finish at all. The race of life can be just as difficult, disappointing, and disturbing at times.

Focus on Finishing

You need to run the race of life with the finish line clearly in mind. Remember, it doesn't matter where you start; what counts is where you decide to finish. If we want to be successful in life, we need to determine what our long-term goals are. It is not how good you look in the starting blocks; rather, it is whether you make it across the finish line.

My life's race began to take on new meaning, and I began to be motivated to do something better for myself. It was time to deal with the other ghost that continued to haunt me — my education.

Meanwhile, I was still fighting for full custody of my son. If I wanted to present a better case to gain custody of him, I would have to go back to school to get my GED. I had tried seven times before, but I didn't have any aspirations to succeed. I dabbled in different GED programs, only to pay the fee and quit after a few days. As soon as I became distressed about not knowing how to do the work, I would just give up. The smallest things would turn me off and trigger me not to go back to class. For instance, if I didn't like the way the teacher looked at me or if I wasn't pleased with the time of day the class was held, I would quit. I wasn't motivated to get my GED because I had neither the inspiration nor the aspiration to do so.

But this time, I had a goal: I wanted full custody of Dévon. In addition, the GED Program at Baltimore City Community College was different from the others I had attended. Finally, there was a GED program that could hold my attention long enough for me to graduate and finish my high-school education. The school provided weekly presentations on various topics by staff members. Visitors from both the financial-aid office and the admissions office also spoke to the students to motivate us to attend college after we received our diplomas.

I was twenty-five years old when I decided to attend class at BCCC, in search of the hope, inspiration, and motivation to get me to the next level of my life. I was tired of having the windows of opportunity slammed close on me because of my lack of enthusiasm. I was tired of limited employment opportunities.

At first it appeared that I would have to wait to enroll. My entry scores were very low, which placed me in the Adult Basic Education (ABE) courses. Even though I'd had trouble filling out job application forms, I was shocked when the test administrator told me my reading skills were on a third-grade level. I thought they were okay, even though most of my school time had been spent playing around and disrupting the class. But the test didn't just measure how well I could *read* the words; it measured how well I *understood* them. Unfortunately, this score meant I couldn't technically enroll in a thirty-day GED class. I would have to finish the six-month ABE courses first. Then I would be tested again. If I my literacy skills were high enough, I would be able to enroll in a GED course. Not wanting to wait six more months, I went to the program director, Mrs. Arah, and pleaded with her to let me into the GED program instead. She finally gave me the okay to take a GED class with several stipulations: I had to promise to attend class every day, to do all the home assignments that were required of me, and to behave like a mature adult in class.

GED classes were a new experience for me. When I arrived at my first class, I was very nervous because I hadn't been inside a classroom in nine years. Even though I'd made a promise to Mrs. Arah about my conduct in class, I immediately regressed to my schoolboy ways of joking around, just as I'd done in high school. But the personality types in the GED class were far different from those I remembered. Most of the students talked about how they had been "A" students until their senior year. Others had been out of school for many years and now had children who had already graduated from high school. Still others were sick and tired of being unable to land a decent job to take care of their families. Then there were those, like me, who initially didn't take their education seriously, and consequently, became disruptive during class time.

One of the teachers, Mr. White, stood out to me because he was young — in his mid-twenties, like me — energetic, and apparently understanding. Students often complained about not learning anything in the Language Writing class. So, Mr. White, who essentially taught math, decided he would teach us both subjects to better prepare us for the exam. The following week, I came to class angry and upset because I was dealing with the frustration of my son's custody battle. During the lessons, I felt Mr. White was picking on me for no reason at all. He would call on me, knowing I didn't know the answers, and I would respond, "I don't know. You know, math just ain't my thang." When he called on me during the writing lesson, I felt enough was enough. Then the question came that I couldn't bear to hear: "Mr. Miller, can you please read the passage?" Although it was just three paragraphs long, to a nonreader like me, it might as well have been three chapters. All the students, who were in the same boat as I, looked at me in anticipation.

As I sat there, knowing I would be embarrassed by my reading skills, sweat began to pour down my eyes from my forehead. Would I pronounce the words correctly? Would I have to guess some of them? Would I stutter while trying to figure them out? Other students began to mumble to themselves, "Man, I wish he'd hurry up and read. D@mn! It's not that difficult!"

Okay, Michael, I told myself, *you can do this!* As I began to read, I stumbled and stuttered over the words. My classmates began to chuckle out loud, as they had done when my third-grade teacher had embarrassed me in front of the class. Once again, the tables were turned on me, and I became frazzled and discombobulated.

Frustrated and angry, I jumped up in the middle of class and yelled, "I'm tired! I'm tired of this crap, and I don't have time for this! I can't read! I can't write! And I sure as hell can't do math!" I slammed down the book and stormed out of the classroom.

The Turning Point

The teacher, Mr. White, followed me into the hallway, and for the first time in my life, I cried out of anger. I usually dealt with anger by keeping everything bottled up inside of me.

Besides, I had tried voicing my opinion, and it didn't work. But that day, I had exploded with emotion.

Mr. White never asked me why I was crying. He just said, "You don't cry much, do you?"

"No, I ain't no punk," I said, wiping the tears from my face. "I don't cry. My eyes are just watery right now."

"Look," he said, "I don't know why you're crying, and I don't need to know why. But I can tell you this, if you apply the same energy from your anger and your tears to your education, you will be very successful one day. I promise you."

That was the moment I decided to take my education seriously. I needed to do better for myself and my son. Instantly, I felt like a new person. I was crazy enough to believe that if I said to a mountain, "Mountain, get out of my way!" it would move. My faith began to revive, and I began to feel good about the person I could become — a scholar — and not the person I was presently — a man without his GED who could barely read.

Unfortunately, many of us focus on who we are and not on what we can become. After that day, Mr. White made a personal commitment to work extra hours with me after class to help me meet my full potential.

A Promise to be Committed

Just as Mr. White made a commitment to work with me, I made a commitment to myself to finish what I'd started and get my GED. Since I had been out of school for nine years, I made a commitment to read and study for nine hours a day, reading everything I could get my hands on, from cooking directions to candy wrappers. Finally, I was able to graduate from reading household items to reading my very first book, *Gifted Hands*, by Dr. Ben Carson. Wow! What an amazing story! Truly inspiring! This book left me speechless. Now here's a guy, who just like me had a temper, came from the ghetto, was a troubled youth, but found the courage to change his life around. Now, he's the world's most sought after neurosurgeons today. And I was inspired to know that if Dr. Ben Carson can come from out of his circumstances and become who he is today, then so can I. His book truly helped me realize that in spite of where you come from or what you're going through, you can make it and be whatever you want to be.

I even carried a pocket dictionary with me wherever I went to look up any unfamiliar words I encountered. I made sacrifices for the betterment of my education: giving up television, hanging out on the corners with my friends, and going to parties all the time were just a few. It was time to stop playing games and deal with those demons that had haunted me for years. I thought changing everything on the outside was the answer. But only when I started dealing with my fears, changing what was on the inside, could I get back into the race and finish everything I had started. We watch what we eat, but never spend the time to find out what's eating us.

Whenever I did have time to watch TV and a person said a word I didn't recognize, I wrote down the word and looked it up in my pocket dictionary. By the end of the day, I would have about thirty or forty new words in my vocabulary. I did the same thing in Mr. White's class. I think he knew I was writing down words, so he used unfamiliar words to challenge me and help me build my vocabulary. I was determined to get out of this rut. Because I was so dedicated and diligent in the pursuit of my education, I made significant improvements in all subject areas within three weeks.

Even though my in-class outburst was the beginning of my commitment to myself to take my education seriously, there were still times when I allowed doubt to set in. The closer I got to my goal, the more nervous I became about finally finishing what I'd started— the achievement of my high-school diploma. Just the thought of it would speed the pace of my heart, and I'd break into a sweat. But in order to face the *demons* of my past, I had to return to the past.

When the time finally came for me to take the state GED examination, I had to force myself to leave my house to take the test. I've always been a person who feared rejection. In fact, this fear was one reason I couldn't finish what I'd started. I didn't want to face the pressure of what might be or could be. I was afraid of failure. Many of us are scared to finish what we've started, because we fear what may happen if we don't succeed. I kept hearing voices of doubt telling me if I didn't do well, I could lose everything — including my hopes, my dreams, and my son. I was scared of going back to my old way of living and barely getting by, but I also feared facing what it would take to complete this mission. The night before the exam, I couldn't sleep at all. I had to keep reminding myself why I was doing this, and who I was doing it for — my son.

If it is to Be, It's Up to Me!

I had relied on my mentor, Mrs. Arah, the program director, to get me this far. The only other constant motivation was my brother, Dennie, who was a mentor to me, as well. He consistently challenged me do to better with my education. He was always a prime example of a self-motivated individual. He was an exemplary brother and mentor. Now it was up to me to use my own internal motivation to inspire myself. I knew I had a lot on the line, so I kept repeating the slogan from a gold plaque on Mrs. Arah's desk, "Just Do It". I told myself, *Michael, if no one else is rooting for you, I am*. Now that I was pumped up and ready to "just do it," I left the house to take my GED examination. By the time I arrived at the testing site, my motivation had died. I was on an emotional roller coaster.

It was mid-October and the building was filled with a morning chill, yet I was sweating bullets. I contemplated quitting the race to avoid finishing what I'd started. My thoughts changed from "Just Do It" to *"Just Do It Later"*. Then I mentally compared the three people cheering me on with the many who weren't. I recalled the words the Baltimore City Unit Chief of Social Workers had said to me: "Mr. Miller, there is no way you will ever get your son again." Out of anger, I had cursed him out. I played back the judge's comment: "Mr. Miller, there is no way you will be able to meet all these requirements in such a short time." My response to him was, "Just wait...You'll see!" I remembered the statistics on people of my economic and educational background, whose chances of passing the GED exam in only five weeks were slim-to-none. I also thought about my so-called friends, who'd had the nerve to tell me it was too late to even try to finish the daunting task of going back to school. My response was, "It's never too late!"

To motivate myself, I thought about the millions of African-Americans who had protested for their right to receive an education in this country. They were spat on, beaten, lynched, and had died to give me the right to drop out of school, live a meaningless life, and go back to school to take a GED exam. I said to myself, "I've got a right to be here!"

I thought about what seemed to be the only statistical data available about the survival chances of Black men, which served as a device for them to lose hope within themselves: "By the age of twenty-five, the average Black man will be either dead, in prison, or under some type of police supervision, scrutiny, or surveillance." As I pondered those statistics and my actual age at that time, twenty-five, I said to myself proudly and boldly, "I must be a survivor!"

Yes, I realized that I hadn't had someone to nurture me and show me how to be a father, but I also thought about the great African-Americans who had made it in spite of all the obstacles they had encountered. I thought about the number of Black fathers walking out on their families and running away from their responsibilities and the rarity of Black fathers actually stepping up to the plate. But I also thought about the untold stories of Black slaves who had escaped slavery, migrated to the north, worked, and then gone back and bought freedom for themselves, their wives, and their children. I thought about the stereotypes, the obstacles, and the perceptions by which modern society views African-American men. And, I remember saying to myself, *Today, I can help change the world's perception of Black men and Black fathers by finishing what I've started.*

Due to my consistent positive self-talk, I empowered myself to take the GED exam. Motivating yourself with positive thoughts can make a difference in everything you do. You need motivation all day, every day. As one motivational speaker once said, "People often say that motivation doesn't last. Well, neither does bathing. That's why we recommend it daily."

As soon as my thoughts finished wandering, the test administrator said to the classroom full of eager GED test takers, "Please put everything away except a pencil. The test is about to begin." The race was on. By the time I had finished taking the exam, there was no one left in the room but the test administrator and myself. When I left, I kept my head up. Even if I didn't pass, *I had finished what I'd started!*

The Big Brown Envelope

Because I had been the last person to finish the exam, I was sure I had failed the test. I didn't want to wait for the test results to tell me I had failed all subjects. I wanted to stay focused, so I immediately re-enrolled in the GED program. One night my buddies, Jay and Sam, came over to my house to pick me up for Jay's birthday celebration. Though I was finished with partying, I thought it was okay. It was my boy's birthday. Jay, who was always nosy, noticed the big, brown envelope on the kitchen table.

"Mike, what's in the big brown envelope? Food stamps?"

I replied, "Nuttin." Just some bad news about school, and I ain't got time to be hearing some bad news right now. I'm focused, my head is on straight, and I *will* get my G.E.D.... some day."

"Man!" Jay said. "Why don't you just open it? You don't even know what the results are."

"Obviously, you *don't* understand. Just an ounce of rejection will take me away from reaching my goal of getting my GED. I'm on a mission."

"Oh, yeah? So that's the way it's going to be, huh?"

"Yep!"

"Well, let's see," Jay said.

"No, no, *no!*" I yelled. "I don't want to know right now, man! I already know what it is, and I'm in my second class right now preparing to take the exam again."

We started tussling over the envelope. Jay held me down while Sam grabbed it and read the results. Sam yelled out, "You passed! You passed! You passed! You've received your Maryland high-school diploma! Man, you got your GED!"

I stood there in shock from the news. Not only had I passed, but I'd passed with extremely high scores. I was astonished and overjoyed. Once again I found myself in tears, breathless, and overcome with emotion. I had waited many years for this moment.

Other than the custody battle for my son, this was another reason for me to believe I could do anything I wanted to do. All I had to do was stay focused. Words can't express the joy I felt that night. I started thinking about all the obstacles I still had to overcome in running my race. I pondered all the jobs I still couldn't get. I remembered my mama kneeling at the foot of her bed and praying that one day all the madness in my life would end and I would get my act together. Tears poured from my eyes as I stood there thinking. The words of Muhammad Ali came into my mind, and, with my voice cracking, I shouted, "I am the greatest!"

We went out to celebrate Jay's birthday after my emotional episode, but mentally I wasn't there. I was still in my living room listening to Sam tell me I had received my Maryland high-school diploma. I couldn't wait to rush home to see and hold the high-school diploma with my name on it.

There was an elegant graduation celebration for all the students who had obtained their GED. This ceremony was a grand occasion that made me feel extremely special. We all had caps and gowns. The men wore dark-colored shirts and ties, while the women were dressed in business suits--just like high-school graduates, only better. Our family members were there to cheer us on. I was even chosen to give a speech as the class representative.

Nontraditional graduations seem to be more emotional than traditional, high-school graduations for both the students and the guests. Although many traditional, high-school graduates have overcome obstacles to earn their diplomas, the nontraditional students have overcome major setbacks, disappointments, heartaches, pains, and struggles to go back to school and finish what they'd started. The emotional triumph is unlike any other. There is nothing like the feeling of opening doors that were once slammed in your face, disproving your critics' claims that you would never make it, and beating the odds stacked against your success. Some students began crying before they even walked down the aisle. They stopped to comfort and congratulate each other on a job well done. I heard many say, "I can't believe I did it!" Many of the guests, having lived through difficult experiences themselves, were also overwhelmed with emotion.

On the surface, I was a composed man—collected and dignified. Inside, though, was another story. I nearly trembled with pride. Pacing myself was difficult—I had to resist the urge to run to the stage and stretch my arms above my head in victory. Looking at my mother was almost too much for me to handle— to see in her eyes what looked like admiration was more than I could've ever asked for. Hearing my name called—Michael ----- Miller—was confirmation that my life had begun.

Following the graduation, we had an elegant reception in the college's cafeteria organized by Mrs. Arah to reward our efforts. She had set up the reception room as if it were a banquet hall. There were elegant bouquets on every table, a jazz band playing while we ate with our families, and caterers wearing black suits and bow ties serving our food. It was one of the proudest days of my life.

Stick!

Although you set your goals, sometimes you may succumb to the temptation to quit or give up. Along with doubting yourself, you'll struggle with every day distractions that will seem to impede your goals. These distractions come in all shapes and sizes and include your family members, your surroundings, and your circumstances. You just have to keep running to reach your goals in the midst of temptation.

During your race, you must keep your eyes on the prize. Great track coaches teach their runners to focus ahead at all times. Certainly, they're aware of the world they're leaving behind, but their concentration is not behind them. If it were, they'd risk becoming distracted and might lose focus as a result. It's important to keep your eyes fixed on the finish line. This will prevent you from losing your stride and your momentum. Use the finish line as your point of reference so that your eyes are always searching forward.

The importance of keeping one's eyes ahead while running was powerfully illustrated during a track meet. There were four teams competing in the 440-yard relay race—the most highly anticipated race of the meet. As the runners for each of the teams blasted out of their starting blocks, they collectively unleashed enough force to move a mountain. At top speed, their hands slashed through the air like switchblades. All four runners were neck and neck as they turned the corner for the home stretch. The winner of the relay race was contingent upon the performance of each team's anchorman. The anchorman for one of the teams mistakenly looked back. As a result, he messed up the timing of the third runner who was giving him the baton and caused a fumbled exchange.

The anchorman for the other team, though, kept his eyes

on the finish line and began slowly building momentum. As he approached the anchorman, the runner of the third leg shouted, "Stick!" which is the call that occurs when the baton is exchanged. Once the third runner hollered, "Stick!" the fourth runner knew to stick his hand back and receive the baton. He did not need to not look back. As a result of this flawless exchange, the third team won the race. The anchorman's ability to keep his eyes focused on what was before him was the key to their victory.

You cannot allow what's behind you to guide you. If so, you'll fumble the baton and lose the race. You must have the *persistence* to go the *distance* in order to finish the race. The third runner is coming around the corner, and he/she is shouting to you "Stick!" When the baton is passed, will you finish the race? Will you give it all you've got? Will you have a strong finish?

Chapter 8

Overcoming the Hurdles:

A Setback is a Setup for Comeback

"So many times, it happens too fast; you trade your passion for your glory. Don't lose your grip on the dreams of the past. You must fight just to keep them alive."

— "Eye of the Tiger", Survivor

hurdle - *noun.* an artificial barrier or obstacle, in which competitors must overcome or leap, in order to win the race.

We will all face our own unique set of hurdles in our lives. Just about all of us will trip over some of them before getting to the finish line. Many of us will get up and run again, eventually crossing the finish line victoriously; whereas, others will trip over the first hurdle and never get back up again. Some will even use their precious time on the track to whine and complain about the fact that they've stumbled over the first hurdle, not understanding that the time clock of opportunity is still ticking. How do I know? Because this is the

151

same thing I did when I was faced with a unique set of hurdles in my life.

Uh, Oh! Another Hurdle!

I now had to face a series of hurdles to win custody of my son. First, the problem was my education, so I went back to school to get my GED and enrolled in college. Then the problem was I hadn't taken any parenting classes, so I went to the Department of Social Services' Young Fathers/Responsible Fathers Program and finished with honors.

It was one roadblock after another. I would do everything they asked of me and more, and still they weren't satisfied. One day, I got so sick of the stupidity that I lost my cool and cursed out the judge, the social workers, and the supervisors. I didn't mean to curse them out. I was doing everything in my power to do what was required of me and none of it mattered. It was the only way I knew to express my anger at that time. After that incident, they all said it would be impossible for me to get my son back.

This was a Job for Superman!

I didn't know a man would have to work so hard to gain custody of his child. There are thousands of cases with crack-addicted mothers who neglect and abandon their children. The Department of Social Service gets involved, but the mothers are most often granted guardianship of their children after completing a thirty-day drug rehabilitation program. Having gone through my experience, I realized it was not that easy for

152

fathers. I knew the battle I was fighting was bigger than I was. Who was I to fight an entire system? As the saying goes, "It's not the size of the dog in the fight, but the size of the fight that's in the dog." They thought they were fighting against me, but they were really fighting against the God in me.

In times like these, I knew that this was a job for Superman! I knew He was the only one who could come to my rescue immediately. As I struggled to get custody of my son, I was always walking by faith and not by sight. The scene was too devastating to watch. But because I had faith, I knew that one day I would get him back, and I made sure I always had the necessary living arrangements just in case.

I'll never forget what the social worker's supervisor told me after I'd cursed out the judge and the social workers. She took it very personally. "Mr. Miller," she said, "you will never get custody of your son. You bastard! I'll see to that. You will never get him. Not over my dead body."

I replied, "Well, if I was you, I would check my insurance policy to make sure everything is okay, because you must be dying. Oh I will get custody of my son! You just wait and see!"

After an emotionally taxing and grueling custody battle that tore me down with rejection after rejection (I was told "no" some forty three times), I won against the entire Department of Social Service, as well as against the court system, with the help of God. Consequently, I was awarded full custody of my son. If I had relied on "reality" or what others perceived as possible, I would have failed long before. The moment I realized I would be taking Dévon home with me, I was simultaneously overcome with a sense of exhaustion and a profound impression of joy—it had been a tedious, sometimes overwhelming battle, but it had been won.

The Next Hurdle-College

My next hurdle that I had to overcome was enrolling into college. Mrs. Arah and Mr. White continued to push me to go further with my education. After repeatedly hearing them tell me they saw great potential in me, I finally decided to take their advice.

To reinforce her faith in me, Mrs. Arah offered me a full scholarship to attend classes at Baltimore City Community College. In the back of my mind, I said, "Nah, not right now. Maybe later." At that time, I was still equally scared of success and failure. Just like so many of us, I made excuses and procrastinated. With Mrs. Arah's constant advice to challenge myself and go beyond the GED and Mr. White's mentorship, I finally began to believe that I could achieve my goal of becoming a college student and someday to graduate. Motivated by their insistence to move to the next level, I made the critical decision to attend college.

Mrs. Arah had an extra reinforcement which persuaded me to go to college. As always, every time I visited her office, I saw the gold plaque that read, "Just Do It." Had it been left up to me, I would've procrastinated further. However, the words on that plaque just kept ringing in my head. It's important, as you strive to reach your goals, to have some slogan to read constantly and remember during your times of weakness.

154

Unfortunately, procrastination often sets in, and "Just Do It" turns into *"I'll Just Do It Later."*

There was another incident that furthered my determination to finish my education. I will never forget the day I first enrolled in college. I was discouraged about attending because I had been out of school for nearly ten years. I kept thinking about how my skills would not be as sharp as the other students.

Mrs. Arah constantly reminded me, "Michael, you can do this! There is nothing different between them and you. As long as they put on their pants the same way you do, you can do anything that anyone else can." After constantly hearing this advice, I finally went to enroll in Baltimore City Community College. I intended to go to college for a semester to see if I liked it and if I would fit in. My approach to this particular goal was very passive. Besides, not too long before, my only goal had been to get a GED to help me get a better job.

Now, I had gained confidence in myself and wanted to go to college to stay out of trouble and out of harm's way. Even though I had worked hard to earn my GED, I still battled with the everyday temptations of hanging on the corners. I still needed additional reinforcement once I started college. My grandmother always said an idle mind is the devil's workshop. So, I had to stop being complacent. I had to be constantly moving, doing something productive with my life to ward off those thoughts of quitting what I'd started.

I decided to enroll in college only one month after receiving my GED. I was still so excited about having my GED that I started walking around telling people I had my PHD: **P**ublic

High school Diploma.

You should've seen me. I had a swagger in my walk. I strolled into college with my thug gear on, confident that I belonged there. My left shoulder was high and upright, my arm close to my side, while my right shoulder dangled downward, arm swinging. I was bopping my way into my destiny. When I arrived at the college, I met with my advisor to go over my academic goals and to pick my major. After our introductions, she went over my transcript and realized I had just received my GED.

I explained that my intention was not to have a major, but to go to school so that I wouldn't be on the streets wasting my life away.

She asked me, "Mr. Miller, how many credits do you plan on taking this semester?"

"Well, that depends," I replied. "How many credits do I need to be considered a full-time student?"

She responded, "You must take at least twelve credits."

I immediately replied, "Twelve credit hours are exactly what I need. I need to stay busy. Can you please enroll me for twelve credit hours, ma'am?"

She shook her head. "Uh, uh, uh. I don't think so!"

Shocked, I replied, "Why not?"

"Well, I think this is a bit too much for you, considering your educational background. Besides, you'll be in the class-room with high school graduates who are fresh out of school."

I pleaded with her to allow me to go to school full time. I began to quote my grandmother's saying, "Ma'am, you must understand: 'An idle mind is the devil's workshop,' and if I don't go to school full time, I may start something I'll regret later. I can do this. Just give me a chance to prove myself. I've partied enough in my lifetime. Now I'm ready to be serious about my education." I wanted to make sure the devil would no longer consider my mind a place to set up shop.

She said, "Mr. Miller, I understand what you're trying to do. But right now, we have to look at what's realistic."

I said, "Realistic, my a_ _! Ma'am, I'm on a mission!"

"Now, wait a minute, Mr. Miller. First of all, you need to watch your mouth."

I replied, "Okay, I'm sorry."

But then she said in a condescending tone, "Mr. Miller, I don't think you should go to school full time. After all, you *only* have a GED, and you just got that!"

I angrily replied, "Ah, no, the hell you didn't! What do you mean, I *only* have a GED?"

Because I lacked a college-level vocabulary, I cursed her out thoroughly to show her exactly how I felt about her comment and the way she had delivered her words. I remember thinking, *It's one thing for someone to try to bring you down when you're not doing the right thing, but it's a crying shame to bring you down when you're trying to live right.* She was trying to downplay my hard-earned accomplishment, as if getting a GED was not of great significance. She was also implying that a GED, unlike graduating from high school, was not an academic honor.

After all my attempts to change her mind, her perception

157

of how she thought I would do in school never changed. She insisted that she wouldn't recommend my entering college full time. It didn't matter to me whether I passed or failed. I knew I would have to live with the outcome. But after I caused chaos in her office, she told me she didn't think I had the right attitude to do well in college. As I walked out of her office, she said, "A college is not a place for thugs like you. You ought to be thankful that you finally got your high school diploma! Go get a job somewhere!"

As a result of her condescension, sarcasm, and lack of understanding, I decided not to enroll in college. I walked away from her office as angry as I had been when I made the outburst in Mr. White's class. Only this time, there was no one there to calm me down and tell me that everything was going to be okay.

I realized that out of all of the condescending things this advisor had said to me, she was right about one thing: I had only just earned my GED. I came to her office with enthusiasm, only to leave with anger. As I left the building, I downplayed the situation to myself, "College ain't for everybody, anyway," I said. All because of what someone had thought of me, I left the school knowing I was going back to the street corners. How could she disparage something I'd worked so hard for? How could she steal the joy I felt before I had walked into her office?

Who's Stealing Your Joy?

My advisor stole my joy and disparaged my accomplishments because I let her do it. No one can do anything to you unless you *allow* them to. If people who are regressing see you are making progress, they may try to stop you because they don't want to see anyone doing better than they are. If you give them the power to hold you back, either physically or mentally, your lack of progress is not their fault but your own. You have handed that power over to them. No one controls *your* destiny except *you*.

Nothing can be stolen unless you leave yourself vulnerable for a thief to rob you of your goods, your joy. Did you leave the front door unlocked or give your house keys to someone who can't be trusted? Was the back door unlocked? Did you put your keys underneath the doormat, thinking a thief wouldn't check to see if someone was stupid enough to put them there? Have you put your faith in man and not in God? A thief always scopes out the scenery first, and if he feels that a house is worth robbing, he will steal all your hard-earned money and possessions — and your joy.

Because I had let someone steal my joy, I decided not to enroll in college, and I went back to a wasteful life of doing nothing. Two months went by, and the first week of the semester was approaching. In desperate need of one of her pick-me-up hugs, I stopped by Mrs. Arah's office to say hello. Her hugs made me feel wanted and appreciated, like a son being hugged by his mother.

After another one of her huge, affectionate hugs, she asked me, "Michael, are you ready for school next week?"

My response was, "Well, there's been a slight change of plans. Instead of following the advice on your desk that says 'Just Do It,' I've decided to wait and just do it later."

159

I described to Mrs. Arah my encounter with the advisor and how the woman had made me feel with her comment about my GED. I told her about how she thought the minimum twelve credits might be too much for a former GED student. I also explained how belittled her comments had made me feel.

"What?" she responded. "You go back to school to register, and you tell her you have the right to take as many credits as you want to take!"

With Mrs. Arah's advice, I went back to school the following day to pay the same advisor another visit. While I was waiting for the advisor to come and meet me, I started mapping out the schedule of courses I wanted to take.

Can a Rose Grow Out of Concrete?

Not only did I take Mrs. Arah's advice, I also took the advice of Tupac Shakur. In an interview on television, he stated:

> "If you walked by a street and you were walking on concrete and you saw a rose growing from concrete, even if it had messed up petals and it was a little to the side, you would marvel at just seeing a rose grow through concrete. So why is it that when you see some ghetto kid grow out of the dirtiest circumstance and he can talk and he can sit across the room and make you cry, make you laugh, all you can talk about is my dirty rose, my dirty stems and how I'm leaning crooked to the side, you can't even see that I've come up from out of that."

I was now prepared to go back and reclaim my joy. Once I was in the advisor's office again, I asked her, "Ma'am, can a rose grow out of concrete?"

She said, "Huh?"

"Please answer the question," I said. "Is it possible for something as precious as a rose to grow out of something so hard as concrete?"

Her response was, "Well, young man, it appears to me that it's not likely for a rose to grow out of concrete."

My response was, "I thought that would be your answer." I just knew she would reject the analogy, just as she had rejected the idea that a young man, such as myself, could defy the odds and be a worthwhile person one day. If you believe that a rose can't grow out of concrete, chances are you believe that a glass is half empty and not half full.

Mrs. Arah had already informed me that I didn't have to agree with the advisor's recommendation regarding college; her recommendation was just that–a recommendation. So, I told her, "Ma'am, *this* rose, which has grown from concrete, would like to enroll for eighteen credits. These are the courses I would like to take this semester."

She looked at me and realized she had no choice but to sign my registration slip, even though she thought I was making a mistake.

After she signed the slip, I grabbed it from her desk. As she grunted to herself and squirmed in her chair, I kindly said to her, "Ma'am, a rose *can* grow from concrete. God may allow rain to come and penetrate the concrete. And once the concrete has been pounded, the water will be absorbed. And then the hard concrete must return to its original state of sand and cement dust, making it easier for the rose to grow, just as easy as it would be to grow in dirt."

She just stared at me with this puzzled look, as if I was crazy, and as if to ask, "What scholar did he get that from?"

So I answered her without even being asked, "Oh, by the way, I got that information from a scholar named Tupac Shakur."

As I walked out of her office and went to the registrar's office to get my printed schedule, I realized the incident had been a blessing, not a curse. Because of her initial rejection, I ended up taking eighteen credit hours instead of twelve my first semester in college. I also made up my mind that I would never give someone that much power over me again. I don't ever plan on relinquishing my power without a fight. Whatever or whoever is stealing your joy and power, take it back!

Shake it Off!

The media had been following my progress as I fought to make something of myself, and they had been kind up until I registered for eighteen credits. I was distraught to learn a headline read: "Michael Miller: Student Bites Off More Than He Can Chew."

It was tough to endure all the media criticism of my decision to take eighteen credit hours. The critics started to pull out statistics to prove that the course load would be too arduous for me. However, the criticism just fueled my drive to excel even more.

I finished that semester with a 4.0 GPA. I wasn't satisfied with using only my first semester to prove my critics and the advisor had been wrong, so I decided to enroll for fourteen credit hours during the summer, twenty-four credit hours during the fall semester, and twenty-one credit hours for the final (spring) semester. All the while I was working full-time and being a single parent.

That experience taught me that I could receive victory in the midst of adversity. This lesson is also clearly illustrated in the story of "The Dog In The Well":

There once was a farmer whose dog fell into a dry well. After assessing the situation, the farmer sympathized with the dog but decided that neither the dog nor the well was worth the trouble it would take to save him. Instead, he planned to bury the dog in the well. When the farmer started shoveling dirt into the well, the dog panicked. But then it dawned on the dog that every time a shovelful of dirt landed on his back, he could shake it off and step up on the rising level of dirt. As shovelful after shovelful fell on him, the dog said repeatedly to encourage himself: "Shake it off and step up! Shake it off and step up!" Soon, the battered and exhausted dog stepped triumphantly out of the well to safety. What he had at first thought would bury him, had benefited him. It was the *way* he handled his adversity.

You Feel Me?

We've all heard, over and over, the common phrase, "You just have to be motivated to reach your goals." That's easy for people to say when they're already motivated. But what do you say to motivate people who don't see their purpose in life and can't seem to get self-motivated? What do you say to a young man or woman who feels as if there is no reason for living? What do you say to someone who feels as if they don't have a purpose? We obviously can't keep using the same approach. It's apparent this old and tired advice is not working. Usually, we argue with them and tell them they just have to find their purpose and get motivated somehow. This is our typical response, but it's also the wrong response. It will only make them more distant from you, because they will feel you don't understand their situation.

"You just have to be motivated," will appear to be a meaningless answer because it's not always that obvious. If they do not receive helpful advice when they come to us for answers, they will turn to someone who will understand them better. Their outlets will eventually be their friends out on the street corners, drugs, alcohol, prostitution, or even violence.

To guide these seemingly lost souls, you must give suggestions that will help them easily understand you. In fact, the most important component in counseling is the psychology of understanding. Young people want to be understood, and not told how to feel or why they need to stop wasting their lives.

We should not disregard what young people are saying simply because we can't understand them initially. We should ask them to clarify the meaning behind their statements so we can properly advise them and guide them to success.

Once we begin to interpret what they are saying rather than criticizing them for using street slang, we will find out that they experience the same things we do, and that it is possible to understand, relate to, and guide them using our own experiences and wisdom.

For example, when young people say things like, "Do you feel me?" or "I can feel that" and "I'm not feeling this person," what they really mean is, "Do you understand me?" or "I understand that" and "I don't understand/agree with this person." These phrases refer to the idea of someone being felt or touched metaphysically, not physically.

Keys to Motivation

To inspire our youth to be motivated, we must give them the formula for motivation, which is Aspiration + Inspiration = Motivation. In order to be self-motivated, you must first have aspirations. Your aspirations are your goals and the reasons for your motivation. When someone or something gave me a good reason to be motivated, it became a lot easier to reach my goals. You have to have something to aspire to and know the reason why you're doing so. My reason for being motivated was my son. I wanted to provide something better for him. Even when I felt like giving up on my son, my reasons for going after him outweighed my negative thoughts. At first my life's purpose was very foggy, until I realized what my aspirations were.

Second, you must have inspirations. Someone or something must inspire you to be great. Daily inspirations are important to become motivated and even to stay motivated. After my graduation, I posted copies of my GED diploma throughout my apartment — in the bedroom, the living room, the closet, and in the bathroom — to remind myself where I had come from and where I was going.

Don't wait for an award ceremony, promotion, friend, or mentor to show appreciation for your work. Take pride in your own efforts on a daily basis. Praise yourself. Continue to overcome your hurdles and keep the end result in sight. Always look at the big picture: your ultimate goal and the benefits that will come with it. These keys to motivation will help to overcome the hurdles in your life.

Whenever athletes run hurdles, they face many obstacles that could cause them to stumble. But the goal is still the finish line, and the focus is on winning the race. The hurdles are simply obstacles to overcome. Those of us who aren't athletes will face hurdles in our race too, obstacles that can trip us up or slow us down while in pursuit of our goals. Though we may fall, we must keep in mind that these hurdles are nothing but *setbacks* that are *setups* for a *comeback*.

Chapter 9

A Leap of Faith:

The Making of A Man—
A Morehouse Man!

"There is an air of expectancy at Morehouse College. It's expected that the student who enters here will do well. It's also expected that once a man bears the insignia of a Morehouse graduate, he will do exceptionally well. We expect nothing less . . . ."
—"The Charge of the Graduating Class of 1961"
Dr. Benjamin E. Mays, President, 1940–1967

leap of faith - *noun.* the act or an instance of believing or trusting in something intangible or incapable of being proved.

Soren Kierkegaard, a Danish philosopher, argued that a significant, religious-belief system should not be based on physical evidence. Instead, meaningful religion requires what he called "a leap of faith," which requires complete trust in God. Kierkegaard's point is that any logical system contains gaps that can only be bridged by a leap of faith, the absolute certainty of truth in the absence of evidence. Since faith can neither be proven nor disproved, a leap of faith is undertaken in a state that Kierkegaard calls, "fear and trembling"

At some point, you'll reach a stage where there aren't any rational reasons for making a move. You'll have to make it without any logical reasons. You'll have to take "a leap of faith."

I decided to take my leap of faith during the Blizzard of 2000. Logically, it wouldn't have made sense to leave Baltimore and drive through a deadly blizzard, with twenty-eight inches of snow predicted. It didn't make sense to leave home, but sometimes logic doesn't make sense. I was bold, confident, and willing to take this leap of faith.

On several occasions, Mrs. Arah proclaimed that I should attend Morehouse College in Atlanta. At the time, the only colleges I was familiar with were local colleges in Baltimore. I wasn't sure what school I wanted to go to initially. I didn't know about any colleges out of state, let alone Morehouse College. But I knew I no longer wanted to go to school in Baltimore. The distractions provided by my friends and life on the street were unquestionable, so I aggressively pursued colleges outside of Maryland.

By this time, I had scholarship offers from more than twenty-five schools. Eventually I narrowed my choices down to Yale, Duke, Johns Hopkins, and Florida State University–all of which were offering some type of scholarship.

Still, Morehouse College had not responded to my application. The only thing I'd received was a postcard stating that they had received my application. They didn't seem to care about all the national publicity I was receiving—from the front page of Black Issues in Higher Education to a listing in Who's Who among Students America. They seemed unphased by the U.S Dept of Education accolades and my GPA. Morehouse was determined to make me wait. To them, I was just another student desperately trying to get in.

Go to "Da House"

I was getting fed up with waiting to hear from Morehouse, so when an inner voice told me to drive to Atlanta, Georgia, I called up my buddy, Ron and told him of my plans. As products of West Baltimore, we had never traveled–physically or even mentally–beyond the Beltway (Interstate 695), much less outside the state. But something kept pulling at me, telling me I needed to go. Although there were severe snowstorm warnings along the entire East Coast, I didn't change my plans. I remember asking myself, "Do I turn back now?" Without hesitation I gassed up the Camry, and my buddy and I headed for Atlanta, seven hundred miles away — in the middle of a snowstorm. It was nine o'clock in the evening and snow had begun to fall. I picked up Ron and my Aunt Dot, who kept us entertained during the trip. Once she knew I was going to Atlanta, she asked me to drop her off at my dad's hometown in Bertie County, North Carolina. That was a big mistake. She was supposed to show me how to get there, but she was too intoxicated.

I didn't know anything about the interstates or the highways. All I had ever known was Baltimore City. By 9:20 P.M., we were on our way to Atlanta. As we got to the tip of Virginia, more snow began to fall, but we kept on driving. Although Ron didn't have a driver's license, I asked him to drive half the distance to Atlanta.

We were planning to be there in twelve hours, by 10:00 the next morning. While Ron was driving, the police pulled him over and asked for his license and registration. I became very nervous and said softly, "Yo, what are we going to do?" He didn't respond. Instead, he gave the police officer his brother's driver license information.

Meanwhile, my aunt was in the backseat, cursing out the police officer, calling him all kinds of names. He asked us to get out of the car, and she continued to curse him.

I said, "Aunt Dot, will you please be quiet? You promised me that if I let you come, you would behave!"

The policeman warned her that if she said anything else, he would lock her up. Instantly she sobered up.

Just when the police were ready to let us go, they began to get a little suspicious about Ron's driver's license story. Before I knew it, they were taking Ron off to jail to officially check his identity. Because of his other unrelated charges, he ended up staying at the Virginia Detention Center for almost a year, before he was finally released.

Again, I asked myself, *Do I turn back now?*

No, I thought, and proceeded as planned.

In the meantime, I was relying on my intoxicated aunt to give me directions to Bertie County, but she was too drunk to remember. I could barely see through the snowy gusts, and I drove around for about three hours before I knew exactly where to go. By that time she was asleep. I continued to drive through that freezing blizzard with no heater. I could barely see, as the snowfall began to get even heavier.

I finally reached Bertie County. After dropping off Aunt Dot, I had to drive all the way across North Carolina to get back to Interstate 95. My heels were freezing, because air was blowing in through the bottom of the driver's side, dented door. I was scared, all by my lonesome, and I felt like turning back. Instead, I humbled my spirit and asked God to be with me on this journey.

Running On Empty

Fourteen hours had gone by, and I was still driving through the gusty winds of the blizzard. But I had to stay focused because my exit–Interstate 85–was soon approaching. When I reached South Carolina, I needed some more gas, so I left Interstate 85 at the next exit and turned onto a dirt road. The gas station was several miles down the road. It was an old store-front gas station, much different from the ones I was used to seeing in Baltimore.

Four White men were standing on the front porch of the service station. One was a deputy sheriff, who was chewing tobacco with a straw in his mouth. After I finished pumping the gas, I politely asked the men, "Excuse me. Can you please tell me how I can get back on 85 going to Atlanta, Georgia?" They didn't respond. They just looked at me with funny expressions on their faces.

Now, I was really pissed off because I knew they'd heard my question. But they continued to ignore me, so I repeated very loudly and clearly, "Excuse me. Can you guys tell me…" Before I could finish, the deputy sheriff responded, "Goddamn it, you in da wrong town, boy. You in da wrong town."

I was scared as hell! They must have been the Ku Klux Klan. Maybe they were still upset with Kweisi Mfume for causing all that ruckus over the Confederate flag. I got in my car and hauled tail on what I hoped was the way back to Interstate 85. Somehow, I made it.

Georgia on My Mind

I finally arrived in Atlanta around 3:30 in the afternoon. A drive that would usually take about eleven to twelve hours had taken me twenty hours, thanks to the blizzard and my poor sense of direction. Although I was exhausted, I felt like Fanny Lou Hammer, who once said, "I'm sick and tired of being sick and tired, but I am in no way tired." At least there was no snow in Atlanta.

When I got to Morehouse College, I was overcome with emotion by the statue of Morehouse alumnus, Martin Luther King Jr., in front of the chapel.

I also saw something I'd never seen in my life: African-American men wearing business suits with crispy-clean dress shirts, neckties or bow ties, and polished dress shoes. They were sharp!

Where I came from, African-American men seldom stood around together unless they were on a corner selling drugs. And even when I did see them together in the 'hood or at a club, they weren't wearing suits. After that inspirational moment, I knew it was really time for me to pursue a college education.

I made my way to the admissions office to talk to Dean Sterling Hudson. My childhood neighbor, Mr. Al, always told me, "Whenever you do business, never talk to rookies. Always deal with the big man." Dean Hudson's assistant informed me that I needed an appointment to see him. She insisted that he had a very busy schedule and wasn't seeing anyone. However, after that long ride, and as determined as I was, I wasn't going to take "No" for an answer.

No matter how much she kept telling me I couldn't see the Dean, I kept insisting that I see him. I told her it would only take a minute.

Before I knew it, a tall, intimidating-looking man came out of his office and said, "What seems to be the problem here, young man? Why are you giving my administrative assistant a hard time, son?"

I said, "Mr. Hudson, I don't think the trouble I'm giving her is as difficult as what I had to go through to get down here. Please, sir, I usually don't beg. I just want a minute of your time."

He replied, "I can only give you one minute. I have a board meeting to attend."

As soon as I stepped into his office, I noticed a copy of the magazine, *Black Issues in Higher Education*. I was featured on its front-page cover. I said humbly, "Sir, my name is Michael Miller."

He said, "I know exactly who you are."

I responded, "I'm going to give it to you straight, no

chaser. I've been awarded scholarship offers to several schools, including Yale, Duke, Johns Hopkins, and Florida State — all except Morehouse College. Sir, the bottom line is I was destined to go to this school. I've come to realize Morehouse is where I need to be. Yes, I have many scholarship offers to many schools, but I need to be here. I can't wait on this decision any longer. That's why I spontaneously drove twenty hours through a blizzard to get here."

He asked, "You really drove through that blizzard?"

I responded, "Yes, sir."

He said, "You must be crazy!"

I said, "I am. I'm also tired, sir. My body is exhausted. I can no longer wait to hear my fate. I'm tired of living the way I've been living, and I want to make a change in my life."

He said, "Okay. Well, how do you plan on paying a hundred thousand dollars to go to Morehouse College, Mr. Miller?"

I said, "Now, that's a good question. Well, I guess Morehouse is going to pay for it. I know this college doesn't offer transfer scholarships, but I'd love to have my matriculation funded by a scholarship from Morehouse College. I can't go back to Baltimore to finish my last semester and worry about paying for Morehouse College. Now, I know you think I'm crazy. That's because I am. Now, what's it going to be?"

He said, "Okay, I'll tell you what; give me till some time next week, and we'll see."

I said, "Ah, ah, no, no. I need to know this right now. I've been stressed out over this way too long, and I don't want to be just another phone call. Can we make this happen? Do we have a deal?"

He said, "You know what, Michael? I like your style. You are very bold, assertive, aggressive, confident, and straight-forward. You've got a lot of heart to come in here and tell a man of my stature what you want. We need more men like you. It's quite evident that when you believe in something, you believe in going after it. Yes. We've got a deal!"

As I walked out the door, he concluded, "And by the way, don't ever let me see you again with your pants hanging off your behind. The next time you come, I want you to dress more appropriately, with a dress shirt, a tie, and a suit. You're going to have to get used to it here at Morehouse College. It's a normal decorum here, son."

I said, "Yes, sir."

I couldn't believe it. Spontaneously driving through the blizzard had paid off after all. I felt like the happiest man in the world. For the first time in my life, I could be assertive and bold and get what I wanted, just like when I was back on the streets.

Thanks, Oprah!: Double for My Trouble

Oprah Winfrey once said, "When you empower a Morehouse Man, you empower the world." Never did I think she would empower me. When I reached the top of South Carolina on my way back to Baltimore, I received a phone call on my cell phone from Jim Henry, the president of the D.C. Morehouse alumni chapter. He said, "Michael, I've got some good news for you. Where are you?"

I said, "I'm in South Carolina, just coming from Morehouse, and I've got some good news for you, too."

He said, "What are you doing at Morehouse?"

I said, "It's a long story. I'll tell you later."

He said, "Well, let me go first. I just got off the phone with someone who's pretty impressed with you. The bottom line is that the generosity of Oprah Winfrey is going to pay for your entire education at Morehouse College."

I said, "You gotta be kidding me."

I pulled the car onto the shoulder and pinched myself to make sure I wasn't dreaming. After that, I couldn't hear a word he was saying. I didn't want to be rude, so I thanked him for calling me and told him I would see him when I got back to Baltimore to thank him in person.

As I sat there, all I could do was ask the question, "Why me? Why would anyone want to invest up to a hundred-thousand dollars on my education?"

Then a voice spoke to me and said, "Why not you?" It was a very overpowering emotional feeling. I'd received double portions for my trouble.

From Boys to Men

The rites of passage at Morehouse College taught me that a male is what you are when you are *born*, but a man is what you have to *become*. I just knew that my age, being a single parent, paying my own bills, and taking care of my manly responsibilities encapsulated my manhood. But while I was a man in training, Morehouse College stressed the importance of not just walking, talking, and looking like a man–I had to *be* a man. I had to think like a man. I had to be educated like a man. And I had to show them I was a man.

Initially, I resented the Morehouse philosophy of what defines a true man. It made me furious, and I was ready to take the next plane back home. I asked myself, *Who are they to tell me whether I'm a man or not? They don't know me! I'm already a man! I take care of myself!* But it was at Morehouse that I learned a boy could become a sperm donor but not necessarily a man or a father. Once I understood the concept of responsibility and the transformation from boyhood to manhood, only then was I able to make the transition into manhood.

At Morehouse, it became important for me to finish everything I had started but failed to complete. Now that I was undergoing my manhood rites of passage—spiritually, educationally, mentally, as well as physically–I had to go back and make everything right. I had to atone for every wrong I had committed and for every person I had harmed. All, not some, of my crooked paths had to be made straight.

In Search of My Destiny

While I was still at Morehouse, I made the bold decision to see if I had fathered any children other than Dévon. I had a strange feeling there was the possibility that I could have another child out there somewhere. Even if they already had an acting father, I wanted to accept my responsibility as a man. To find out if I had any other children, I sought out every woman I could have potentially made children with, and I ordered

DNA tests.

I believed that to *reach* my destiny, I had to *find* my destiny. Until I fulfilled my desire to know if I had any other children, I felt incomplete.

Many men get this notion but choose to ignore it. We go on with our lives as if we hadn't left anything behind — even children. We pretend to be happy, but we're not whole. We run away from the truth. How can we claim to be fathers and men while ignoring the possibility that we may have more children who we haven't acknowledged? We're just running from the responsibility and financial obligations that come with raising children. We complain about the little bit of money we send the mothers for child support, worried that we can't afford the car payments or the mortgage payments, but we still dress like we want to. Making a difference in a child's life is far more important than what we drive, where we live, or what we wear on our backs.

Many people told me I was just asking for trouble searching for my abandoned children. A former girlfriend, Rhonetta, initially put up a fight. She stated on several occasions that her son's father was also her daughter's father. Although I didn't know the daughter's name, I continued to fight to see if I was actually her father.

A few years later, I found out that the young girl's assumed father had died, and this was the perfect time to try to convince Rhonetta to arrange a DNA test to see if I was the biological father. After years of trying to convince me that I wasn't the father, she finally gave in. The Circuit Court of Baltimore City warned me that if the girl wasn't my child, I would still have to pay for all the DNA fees and other costs associated with bringing this case before the court. And if she was my child, I would have to pay the past child-support payments and medical expenses which had resulted from her mother being on welfare for the past few years. It was roughly fifteen-thousand dollars, but again, I didn't care. All that mattered was a little girl could be growing up without a dad. I needed to know if I was her father.

On the day of my court hearing, a woman walked into the courtroom. The little girl with her stopped what she was doing and began to gaze into my eyes. We stared at each other for about ten seconds. Then she started smiling. She was cute, cuddly, and chubby. I said to myself, *What fool in his right mind would neglect a precious little girl like this? He must be crazy. Can't he see she needs all the support she can get?* I really felt sorry for this little girl because of the condition she was in. And this did not stop me from having a friendly conversation with her.

I took her hand and asked her, "What's your name?"

"Destiny," she said.

I looked down at my court papers and saw that the little girl in my court case was named Destiny, too. I thought, *This can't be her. She's already with her mother. Oh well, What a coincidence. I'll play with her anyway.*

We had a lot of fun, laughing and playing together for about fifteen minutes. We were having a good time! As I continued to have fun with her, it saddened me to know that her real dad would be coming soon to take her away. I handed her back to the woman she was with. The moment I handed her back, though, it felt like I was surrendering a piece of me. Oh how I dreaded letting that little girl go. A piece of me was now gone. That moment once again reaffirmed the importance of my mission.

Moments later, Rhonetta walked into the courtroom and said, "Oh, hi, Mike. This is Destiny, and this is my sister, Cherita."

I said to myself, "I've found my Destiny!"

As soon as my case came up, the judge declared that I was indeed the father of Destiny, based on the DNA evidence (99.98 percent). I immediately left the courthouse and took her shopping. I began fulfilling my role as her dad. Unfortunately, Destiny's mom had not been seeing to her welfare. Destiny's hair wasn't being combed, and her hygiene wasn't being tended to.

Reclaiming My Destiny

Rhonetta's home and neighborhood was rampant with drugs and, in my opinion, not conducive for raising a child. So, I decided to fight for custody of my daughter, as well. This custody battle was not as difficult as the one had been for my son. Rhonetta had other issues going on in her life that made it a lot easier to win custody of my daughter. A couple of years later, I was awarded full custody of Destiny. Now, I was a single parent of two children.

Raising my daughter as a single parent was a bit more challenging than raising my son. I had to be more affectionate and less militant. Although having a son called for affection and attention, I had to give Destiny more hugs, more kisses, more cuddling, more "I love you, baby." You know, all of that mushy stuff.

I must admit: The new "daddy" in me is changing, for the better. As a single father, I thought raising my *son* to be a *man*, was a struggle. *Naw, not quite.* Raising my *daughter* to be a *young lady* is taking me to new heights and zeniths of parenting. It is much different! Therefore, my plan of action had to change while raising my daughter. Life has taught, and continues to teach me, that with little girls, you have to be more affectionate, loving, and caring—attributes that all fathers will have to learn and achieve in order to affectionately be called, "DADDY!"

Furthermore, raising my daughter, Destiny, and being a father to Brianna is teaching me how to love a woman, more. How? Because when you love a girl, which is the black woman's most infancy state, you reap the early teachings and benefits that one must learn in order to love a woman. Why? Because little girls, just like women, need attention, love, and must be shown affection daily. If not, you run the risk of losing her to the dangers of the world, *forever!* A risk that *no man* can afford to take!

Adam, Adam, Where Art Thou?

According to researcher, Sonora Dodd, "Fathers play crucial roles in their children's lives. Ideally, they teach them love, respect, and discipline. A father's relationship with his daughter is often the best predictor of whether she will grow up to have a lasting, fulfilling relationship with her own spouse. A father's relationship with his son is critically important to the development of self-discipline and a healthy, respectful attitude toward women."

Children whose fathers are involved in their lives tend to do better in school, are less prone to depression, and are more successful in relationships.

Some fathering advocates would say that almost every social ill faced by America's children is related to being fatherless. As supported by the data below, "Children from fatherless homes are more likely to be poor, become involved in drug and alcohol abuse, drop out of school, and suffer from health and emotional problems. Boys are more likely to become involved in crime, and girls are more likely to become pregnant as teens."

According to a study conducted by the U.S. Department of Health and Human Services in 2004, a father's absence is often accompanied by psychological consequences for his children, which include "higher-than-average levels of youth suicide, low intellectual and educational performance, and higher-than-average rates of mental illness, violence, and drug use." Sixty-three percent of teen suicides are related to the absence of a father. Ninety percent of all homeless and runaway children are related to the absence of a father. Seventy-five percent of all adolescent patients in chemical-abuse centers come from fatherless homes. As these disturbing statistics show, it is important for fathers to be there for their children.

I remember when Dévon first came home to live with me. He misbehaved in ways many eight-year-old children do–he was lying, stealing, and being disruptive in school. Realizing that providing for him was not enough, by second nature, I began to raise him as I had been raised, and doing what my parents did.

I wouldn't tell him why I was punishing him. Whenever he acted up, I would just spank him or holler at him, hoping the punishment would teach him to behave. But just as I had perceived the spankings as someone there to *beat* me but not *teach* me, he thought I was just hurting him.

I was just imitating what my parents, who believed "Spare the rod, spoil the child," had done to me. I thought these principles were instructed by God. But that phrase is nowhere in the Bible. I couldn't even find a biblical verse that was close to it. It was just a cliché. What the Bible does say is that constant discipline is the key. Proverbs 13:24 says, *"He who spares his rod hates his son, but he who loves him disciplines him promptly."*

Like my parents, I had good intentions, but I was using the wrong technique. An old adage in the African-American community says, "Everything ain't for everybody." Clearly, beating Dévon wasn't working for either of us, so I began trying other alternatives, beginning with hugging, to show him I loved him.

A Piece of the Puzzle

A father had just settled into his recliner on Sunday afternoon, looking forward to reading through his newspaper, when his five-year-old son, Pookie, came into the room.

"Daddy! Daddy!" said the boy, "Can you play with me?"

The father responded in a calm manner, "Son, Daddy

wants to read his paper for a little while. But if you come back in twenty minutes, we can play together."

Pookie then grumbled as he left the room, leaving his dad alone to read his paper. But five year olds have a poor sense of time. It was only a few minutes before Pookie came back and asked, "Daddy, can we play now?"

"Not now, Pookie," said the father. "Don't bother me until I'm finished reading my paper." Pookie stomped his way out of the room to wait, but before his dad could even get to the sports section, Pookie returned. He pushed his head up under the paper and said, "Please, Daddy, can we play now?"

Now convinced that he would never get a moment's peace without giving in, the father looked on the floor and observed a full-page map of the world included in his newspaper. With scissors, he started to cut the map into many pieces. He then took his son to the kitchen table, grabbed the scissors and some tape, gave it all to his son, and said, "Since I know how much you like jigsaw puzzles, I'm going to give you the world all cut into pieces so you can repair it all by yourself. When you finish putting together the puzzle of the world, then I'll play with you." He knew it would take his son a long time to put the puzzle together, giving him plenty of time to read his paper.

Not five minutes had passed when his son burst back into the room with, "Daddy, Daddy, I'm through with the puzzle! Can we play now?"

"What? You're finished already?" asked the father.

He got up from his chair and went into the kitchen to look. Indeed, the puzzle was complete, with every piece in its

184

proper place.

"Son, how did you do this so fast? You didn't know where the world was. How did you do it?" The father was astonished.

The child answered, "It was easy, Daddy. I didn't know how the world was supposed to look, but on the back of the map was the shape of a man. So I turned each little piece and decided to put the man together first. When I had fixed the man, I turned it to the other side, and the whole world seemed to fit right into place."

The world we live in is, indeed, broken and urgently needs to be put back together. The only way to put a broken world together is by putting broken men back together. Adam, Adam, where are you? If you change your life, men, it will result in a changed world. And when men begin to put their lives back together, the whole world will seem to fit right into place.

Chapter 10

Faith:

How I Got Over

"Faith is like electricity. You can't see it, but you can
see the light."

—Anonymous

faith - *noun or verb.* belief that does not rest on logical
proof or material evidence.

F aith in God was the foundation of my parents' determination to keep our family together and to raise
each and every one of us on their own. Many neighbors talked
about us, laughed at us, teased us, and misunderstood us. But
in the end, they stood in awe of us. They looked at us in shock
and confusion as if to say, "I don't know how they did it." Even
today, we're known as "The Miller family that made it."

All of my brothers and sisters are high school or college
graduates, successful in their careers, and happily married. To
their great credit, my parents raised all of us without the aid of
welfare or after-school programs. They didn't lose a single
child to drugs, and not one of them ever spent a night in jail.

187

According to modern social scientists, we were doomed to failure, but by the Grace of God we beat the odds. Let the social scientists tell it and we were supposed to be a dysfunctional family that handed over six more African-American men to the prison system, and hailed three African-American women with a slew of children without the means to provide for them. Not one of us succumbed to any such path. Instead, my siblings are raising healthy children who are doing exceptionally well.

Had it not been for the Grace of God and my parents' steadfast faith, there's no telling where we would have ended up. My mother would kneel at the head of her bed and call out the name of the Lord, fervently asking God to protect us, lead us, and guide us during desperate and thriving times. As a deacon in our church, my father always made sure he said a personal prayer for his family during altar call. My parents' strong religious faith led me to believe that "trouble won't last always." Even when I went astray, I knew my parents were praying for me. Even when I cursed God, out of anger, I still believed He existed. This faith played a major role in my life. I was always God-conscious throughout my transgressions.

Prayer Does Change Things

Remember from Chapter three when I asked, *"Does prayer really change things, or is it all a hoax?"* Well, my mothers' prayers were finally manifested years later.

Years later, my life began to change for the better—from

188

being a troubled youth, a father at fourteen years old, and a high school drop-out to being called Dr. Miller. I later asked my mother, "Mom, why did God take so long to answer your prayer?"

She looked at me with a smile and said, "Michael, God answered my prayer the first day I prayed. It was just ten years later when it was manifested."

Though she didn't routinely grab us by our hands and pray, my mother often knelt down at the head of the bed to pray for her children. I believe her prayers are the only reason why my brothers and sisters and I have made it this far in life.

One of the key components of faith is optimism. Many times, people subconsciously heal themselves without even realizing it. They'll say things like, "I'm going *through* hell." The key word is *through*. You're going *through* hell; you're not *in* hell. While you're going *through* hell, just keep going. You'll soon get to your destination.

Many of us try to overburden ourselves with issues that are bigger than we are. The race you're running may be going at a faster pace than you expected. Don't rush; just pace yourself. We need to learn how to wait for our circumstances to manifest itself out so that we'll know how fast to run our race.

After being fired by Notre Dame, the first African-American coach, Tyrone Willingham, said, "I have never had a bad day. I have had bad moments, and sometimes, those bad moments will run into another day — okay? — that'll have hurt, pain, etc. But it's still a good day. There are many blessings that Tyrone Willingham has."

Your faith will help you to overcome many obstacles in

your life. It's very important that you not yield to your *feelings* but rely on your *faith*. For example, when someone asks how you feel, say to them, "I don't live by feelings; I live by faith." And your faith throughout your journey in life will see you through.

Nelson Mandela went from being a *prisoner* to being a president, all because he had faith. Benjamin Banneker built and laid out Washington D.C. as if it was a Masonic temple, all because he had faith. Harriet Tubman led thousands of slaves to freedom through the Underground Railroad, all because she had faith. Mary McLeod Bethune went down to a junkyard in Daytona, Florida, and said, "I'm going to build me a college here." Now Bethune-Cookman College is one of the leading African-American institutions, all because Mary McLeod Bethune had faith.

Give It to God

Your life's mission can't be completed by human power alone. At some point during your life's race, you will have to rely on God to make it through your difficult and arduous journey. In fact, that's the ONLY way to make it through. You will have to trust and believe that if God allowed you to go *to* it, He will bring you *through* it. He will equip you with everything you need in your race. You just have to rely on Him. In other words, where God *guides*, He *provides*. He can take a talent, an opportunity, a skill, or a hobby and use it as part of your life's mission to help other people, but you've got to rely on Him.

You may say, "Mike, it's too late for me!"

My response is simple: The race isn't over yet. It's never too late. It's not how you start the race that matters, but how you finish. Keep the faith in your race. Surely, your faith will see you through to completion!

You Gotta Have Crazy Faith!

My experiences have taught me that while you're on your journey in life, it's all right to be crazy. In the race of life, you often worry about how many people are in front of you, how you look, your facial expressions, or how many miles you have to go. If you're crazy, you won't worry about stuff like that. In fact, I think insanity is worrying about something you have no control over, anyway.

You must let God do what He says He's going to do, regardless of how bad the situation may seem. Very soon, He will step in and work things out in your favor, if you believe. Learn how to be a little crazy sometimes, to go by what you can't see yet still believe deep within your heart, even if everyone around you says it isn't possible. You will have to go against the grain of what society determines you can and cannot do.

Unfortunately, we live in a society that prides itself on research data, rather than on the willpower of human beings working collectively with spiritual power. If research dictates that it's impossible, we're left to believe it cannot be done. If no one has done what you're trying to do before, or if it's not thought of as "humanly possible," it may seem impossible for you to reach your goal, mainly because we live in a society that lacks spirituality.

There was a story about a woman in California whose car flipped over on a slippery road. Consequently, her infant son was pinned beneath it. The 3,700 pound car was no match for her love, though. Defying all odds, she lifted the car with all of the "crazy faith" she possessed, and her son crawled from under the car to safety. Though it didn't make logical sense, given the size of her frail body frame, her insanity helped her in her desperate time of trouble. It was a life-or-death situation. When it came to saving her beloved son, her mind gave her body the willpower, resilience, and might of many men.

There are many people who have benefited from using their insanity in a sane society. If they'd had an ounce of doubt or had used their "sanity," they would have failed a long time ago. Instead, they channeled their energy to concentrate on developing the necessary power to endure unbearable circumstances.

Insanity has several definitions. According to Einstein, "Insanity is doing the same thing over and over again and expecting different results." Another wise man once said, "Only the insane have strength enough to survive. Only the survivors determine what is sane."

I'm Crazy!

Had I listened to the teachers, naysayers, and friends who said I couldn't make reality conform to my views, my dreams would have been shattered. Instead, I went through a period where I just went crazy. Quite frankly, I'm still crazy, which isn't a bad thing. I simply realized you've got to exercise mind over matter, because once you lose your mind, nothing else matters.

I was crazy enough to go inside a class

of the students were fresh out of high scho

overcome illiteracy just two months before er

I was crazy to declare, against my advisor's

that I was not only going to graduate with my Associate of Arts degree, but that I was going to do it at the record pace of a year and a half, with honors–a goal that seemed impossible, especially for a student with my background.

After surmounting the obstacles at BCCC, I was crazy enough to consider taking on the challenge of going to the prestigious Morehouse College in Atlanta, Georgia — where my critics said I wouldn't have the same support that the community college was giving me. They said I'd be on my own.

As the haters continued to criticize me for biting off more than I could chew, I responded, "I'm hungry!"

People used to say things like, "Why not go to a local school? Why do you have to be such a big shot and take a risk like that? You're setting yourself up for failure." I remember when one college president, whose school was not one of my top choices, called me and tried to recruit me for his university. When I told him my final choices, he said, "Mr. Miller, it's better to be a big fish in a little pond than to be a little fish in a big pond." I guess I was supposed to respond with fear, take the shortcut, and settle for second best. But instead of giving in, I said, "Sir, it doesn't matter, because I love to swim."

At times, I was crazy enough to take twenty-four credits in a single semester. But, the obstacles I was surmounting weren't about me–they were about the next generation of

193

dents who came along with pasts similar to mine. I challenged myself to give them hope that they could do it too.

I had the same routine every day. I would go to school, go to work, come home and be a single parent, study, check my goal sheet to make sure that I was on track, pray, and then go to bed. I wasn't missing out on anything by giving up my old lifestyle. The people who were in the clubs before I went to college were the same people in the clubs when I graduated. So, it wasn't like I was really missing anything at all.

Only an insane person does things over and over again, and I was not the least bit interested in keeping my sanity. Being sane would have forced me to declare my goals were impossible and that I couldn't do what I had set out to do. I didn't even want to be around sane people. Sane people look at what is real or possible and I didn't care about that.

If you want to finish your race, be crazy! Be crazy enough to have faith when things look bleak. Be crazy enough to walk by faith and not by sight. Be crazy enough to believe your condition is not my conclusion. Be crazy enough to still believe that even in your darkest, most dismal, most difficult destitution, everything is going to be okay. You have to be crazy enough to believe that. If not, you'll walk by *feeling* instead of walking by *faith*. You'll faint where you should have *fortitude*. Instead of believing you have divine *favor*, you will believe you are a *failure*. Soon, and very soon, you will learn that the only thing you need in the face of adversity is faith. That's it!

New Level, New Devils

With each new lap of your race, you may suffer increased attacks that will test your faith. With each new blessing, spiritual attacks seem to increase. When God takes you to a new level, there will always be new challenges and obstacles in your way. Once you move to a new level in your life, there will be more obstacles which will come against you. As you settle into your new place and face new types of adversity, remember your path to your destiny has already been determined.

The curious thing is when I was wasting my life away, nobody cared. But, as soon as I decided to do something with my life, I instantly came under attack from those "new devils." As I moved from having my GED to attending a two-year college, there were naysayers who said, "Michael is going to school? Oh, he's not going to finish. He won't stay in for long. As always, he'll drop out soon."

Some were even bold enough to say directly to my face, "Michael, how are you going to go to college when you've been out of school all these years? Why are you going to embarrass yourself like that? How can you have the nerve to be in a class-room with a bunch of high-school graduates?"

I responded boldly and confidently, "Go ahead, keep talking." And while they were *talking*, I was *walking* into my destiny. When I started taking courses at Baltimore City Community College, I had newer devils. Colleagues and co-workers would congregate and attempt to kill my resilient spirit.

I once heard someone say, "The only reason he's doing

well here is because this is a community college. He'll never do that at a four-year college, especially an honors institution like Morehouse College."

My response? "Keep talking!"

I then went to Morehouse College to continue my matriculation. While I was there, I was inspired by the words of Dr. Mays, "You've got to run *twice* as fast or forever be left behind." And that was exactly what I did. I graduated from Morehouse, too, at a record pace of a year and a half with honors.

Just when I thought I'd done enough to shut my lower-level devils up, there were always new devils coming along, finding something new to talk about, "Well, he has his Bachelor's Degree from Morehouse College, but he can't do it in grad school."

And as always, I would respond, "Keep talking!"

I continued to study at other prestigious universities on a graduate level. Even after receiving my Master's and my Doctorate degree, some new difficulty would always present itself. You would think the critics would realize by now that the more they have to say, the more they motivate me. Scholars of rap music call it "Making your haters your motivators."

As I climbed the ladder, I had to learn how to move on from "Keep talking" to "This, too, shall pass." There is a story about a poisonous snake that crawled into the cockpit of a plane before takeoff. The passengers were alarmed, but the pilot didn't seem to be worried about the snake. He ignored the passengers' concerns and kept flying the plane to higher altitudes. To the passengers' surprise, the snake was dead. The pilot explained that if he flew the plane high enough, the snake would perish. The reptile couldn't tolerate the higher altitude.

After flying higher and higher, you'll notice that, at some point, the snake must die. As you continue to fly, take the time to thank your critics for their tenacious efforts to bring you down. Thank them for their jealousy, their envy, and their deceit. You'll need it to push you to the next level. It will only serve to make you stronger as you climb the ladder of success. It will only be fuel to your faith.

Find a Reason to Run

And finally, you've got to find a reason to *run*—a reason to *succeed*. Find a reason why you're running your race. So, when life knocks you down, when you run out of money, when things don't work out for you, what are the reasons that you can think of that will keep you in the race; that will be your rod and staff that will comfort you; that can be your bridge over troubled waters. Niche' once said, "If you can know the why, you can endure any how."

So, find a reason that will make you pursue your dreams when everybody else is against you. When things happen that you couldn't anticipate, tell yourself, "I'm doing this for my children." Me, personally, I'm doing this because all my life, I've had teachers say, "Mrs. Miller, why bother? He ain't worth it, just give up on him! He's not gonna make it!" But I believe what Frank Sinatra once said, "The best revenge is massive success!"

Chapter 11
The Journey of Self-Discovery:
Where Do I Go From Here?

"When I discover who I am, I'll be free."
—Ralph Ellison

self-discovery - *noun.* the act or process of achieving understanding or knowledge of oneself.

When I finally realized I was destined to win the race of life, I set out on a joyful journey to discover who I really was. I'm reminded of a story told of a man who lost his keys. He had misplaced them while inside his house but decided to look for them outside. As he searched through the bushes and grass, a neighbor came by and asked, "Have you lost something?" The man told his neighbor the state of things and asked if he might help him find the keys. After some minutes of searching and finding nothing, the neighbor asked him, "Are you sure you lost them here?"

The man replied, "No, I didn't lose them here."
The neighbor asked, "Well, where did you lose them?"

The man replied, "Inside the house."

"If you lost your keys inside the house," asked the neighbor, "why are you looking for them out here?"

The man responded, "Because it's dark inside my house. There's more light out here."

The moral of the story is this: the keys to your life will not be found in the light of the world, but in the darkness of your soul. Acknowledgment of your dark side ushers forth light. Besides, the darkroom is necessary for any good picture to be developed.

To discover yourself and ultimately to become whole, you must acknowledge and accept your dark side. No matter what you've done in the past, you can change your behavior today. You did the best you thought you could; now it's time to do better and finish what you've started. To begin, you must visit the dark places in your life.

I tried to avoid writing this book for more than six years. I didn't want to confront the dark areas of my life. When I first attempted to write this book, I was met with great resistance from within myself. It was a difficult and tedious race from start to finish. I had to conjure up old feelings about my past. I'd write a single sentence and walk away because I was so overwhelmed. Eventually I was writing entire pages, but with each I'd have to walk away crying, compose myself, and then go at it again. At times I'd stop writing altogether, attempting to run away from the pain. It was a brutal, painful, arduous battle. But eventually, one agonizing paragraph after another, my pages numbered in the hundreds and I had finished my race...I had written this book!

The Manifestation of My Problems

I've finally realized, through self-discovery, that the things I thought were my problems really weren't my problems. Hanging out on the corners wasn't my problem. Not being a father to my son wasn't my problem. My tragic childhood wasn't my problem. Partying all the time, smoking marijuana, drinking alcohol, and being disruptive in school weren't my problems. Anger certainly wasn't it. Nor was low self-esteem or even my rage against God.

These were simply manifestations of my problems. I had to deal with these manifestations from the inside out.

My problem was that I couldn't set myself free, and I couldn't set myself free because I'd never really known who I was. I thought I was *hard*, but I was really crying out for *help*. I thought I was a *thug*, but I was really a *thinker*. I thought I was a *man*, but I was still only a *male*. Once I was able to change my childish and juvenile mind-set, I was then able to change my self-concept.

R-E-S-P-E-C-T

Far too often, too many of us place being *accepted* over being *respected*. Being accepted is fine, but if we have to compromise being respected, we should reject the idea of acceptance. If we're not free to be who we are, then attempting to be accepted is an act of self-betrayal. Nothing or no one should be that important. Respectfully, I hope and pray that you'll choose the latter.

Self-Worth

Some years ago, a movie entitled The Elephant Man told the story of a man named John Merrick. Merrick was born with a disease that physically deformed him. He was extremely grotesque, with skin like that of an elephant (hence his nickname, The Elephant Man). Doctors could find neither a cause nor a cure for his condition. One day, while Merrick was walking through the tunnel of a London subway, someone spotted him, and he soon found himself running away from a crowd that wanted to see this "thing." They chased him, until he came to a wall and could run no further. Merrick yelled out, "Stop and leave me alone! I am not an animal! I am a human being! I . . . am . . . a . . . man!"

And that, my dear friends, is it. No matter how tall or short we are, no matter how dark or light we are, no matter how skinny or fat we are, we are human beings and not things. A man is a man, not a breadwinner. A woman is a woman, not a piece of meat. A boy is a boy, not a bad little S.O.B. A girl is a girl, not a fast little whore. All of us are God's precious children, made in His image and after His likeness.

Changing Your Self-Concept

Change is very uncomfortable, so you must get comfortable with being uncomfortable. Changing your self-concept will be painful. A battle will commence between the "old you" and the "new you". You'll also struggle with those people you once bowed down to because you'll be speaking your mind and standing up for yourself. And they'll accuse you of thinking you're better than everybody else, and make comments like, "Who do you think you are?....You think that you're a cut above the rest. You think you're all that and a bag of chips" or "You think that you're God's gift to the world."

Actually, you are! You are all that! The Bible declares, "You are a royal priesthood, a chosen generation." You are a child of the Most High, the King (God). Hence, you are an heir to the Throne. If you are a child of the King, then you are, indeed, a Prince or Princess.

Some people will try to bring you down because of their own self-hatred, but you must remain steadfast. When I started standing up for myself and what I believed in, the people around me started feeling uncomfortable because they had become so comfortable with the old, silent me. Remember, we teach people how to treat us, and we must also teach them how not to treat us.

Who you are is not predicated on what other people think of you. Who you are is not reflected in your address or the community you live in. You are not your last name or what you used to do or whether or not you had a father in the house. Who you are is predicated on understanding that you are a child of God. That's it!

Being a child of God indisputably qualifies you as wonderful, regardless of what the world says. My mother used to say it plain and simple, "I am what I am. I is what I is. And I'm gonna be what I'm gonna be. Not because of *who* I am, but because of *Whose* I am!"

Are We There Yet?

Every parent who has taken a long journey with a child is familiar with the question, "Are we there yet?"

Like those impatient children, I was on a journey, but I was not *there* yet. I was *better*, but I hadn't yet reached *best*. Most people are so glad to be *better* that they give up on being their *best*. They fail to take advantage of the opportunity for true greatness because they settle for mediocrity and are often afraid to think outside the box.

"Well, I'm better," they say to themselves, "and *something* is better than *nothing*. At least, I'm making ends meet. At least I'm getting by."

And they're right. They are getting by. But "getting by" is not better, it's second best. I do not believe God has brought us here to "get by."

Don't Worry, Be Happy!

Too often, we choose to worry rather than choosing to be happy. The word *'worry'* comes from the Old English word *'wyrgan,'* which means 'to strangle.' Many times, we worry or "strangle" about things we shouldn't worry about. My mother used to tell me, "It ain't no use putting up your umbrella till it rains."

As long as I've got an umbrella in my hand, which is God, I have nothing to worry about, because I'm protected. He will shelter me from the rain. The Word of God encourages us to avoid worrying about our physical needs like clothing and food. I believe worrying is a sin, because when you worry, you doubt God's capabilities. When you worry, you unconsciously diminish God to someone who can do *some* things, but not all. God will dispatch angels in a time of need, and because He knows our struggles, our pain, and our needs, we need not worry about anything. We're in His Hands.

Your self-concept is also affected by your concept of happiness. Many people believe that if they can change their friends, spouse, or peers, they can enhance their self-esteem, and consequently be happy. I take the simple approach: No one can make you happy; that's your responsibility.

When someone else determines your happiness, you have given him or her too much power and undue influence over you and your unconscious mind. That is too much power for anyone to have. When you are not doing what you want to do, you start to feel helpless, hopeless, and victimized. This causes you to be frightened and angry. Consequently, your happiness has been put on hold.

Dr. Charmaine Sanders writes:

"Happiness lives within us, never outside of us. Therefore, it cannot come from external sources. The joy we get from things outside is the cream on the cake, an extra bonus, but it can never be the whole story. Relying on people, places, or events to make us happy is the ultimate fantasy. It can only bring transitory pleasure and disappointment in the end."

Where do I go from Here?

The journey of self-discovery can be a daunting task at times, but you must be persistent to find which way to go. In the book, *Alice in Wonderland*, Alice comes to a fork in the road. While she stands there looking confused, the Cheshire cat grins facetiously, as if he knows something she doesn't.

She asks the cat, "Would you tell me, please, which way I ought to go from here?"

"That depends a good deal on where you want to get to," says the cat.

Alice responds, "I don't much care where."

To which the cat replies, "Then it doesn't matter which way you go."

Possibly, like Alice, you are seeking a purpose and a direction. As you approach any of several crossroads in your life journey, you may ask, like Alice, which way you should go. But if you don't know where you're going, it really doesn't matter in which direction you go.

You must continue to find "which way to go" in order to achieve your ultimate destination. We can no longer sit around and wait for things to happen...we've got to make them happen!

I've learned that life is filled with crossroads that lead to many destinations, each unique in its own right. Like Alice, I've reached a crossroads, or rather, many crossroads. Unlike Alice, however, I now know where I'm going and the road I must take.

After dropping out of high school, I embarked on an

expedition that led me to college. The road to college led me to a remarkable educational experience. My education at Morehouse College exposed me to some of the greatest minds in the world. During this time, I was forced to answer questions that stimulated my intellect. Confronting and overcoming this challenge took me to other roads that I eventually had to cross.

Ralph Waldo Emerson once said, "Don't go where the path may lead; go instead where there is no path, and leave a trail." College has both challenged me and prepared me for the roads ahead. On the road of life, I am trying to leave a trail, become a compassionate leader, and become a good parent. My college experience took me a step closer to these goals.

Without goals, we are just like Alice — traveling without a purpose in life. Remember, a goal without a plan is nothing but a thought. As one scholar has said, "Those who fail to plan, plan to fail." We all have an innate gift which was given to us. We just have to continue to discover who we are and find out what our life's purpose. We all have one.

In his book, *Live Your Dreams*, Les Brown wrote, "The richest place on the planet is not some diamond mine or oil field. It is a cemetery, because in the cemetery, we bury the inventions that were never produced, the ideas and dreams that never became reality, the hopes and aspiration that were never acted upon." Les Brown also acknowledged that most people take their dreams to the grave because they are afraid. They don't feel worthy, or they listen to negative inner conversations instead of creating their own circumstances for success and exercising the power to change their lives. However, if you block those voices from entering your mind, as Les Brown suggested, your talents — no matter how limited or undeveloped — will take you many places. Places you've never been before.

I once heard a minister say, "God repositions His presence." When He's up front, he *guides* you; when He's in the back, he *guards* you. Before He released you to your destiny, He directed you. When He saw that you were on the right track, He got behind you to guard you. Often, our circumstances can be so overwhelming we can't see God. If God's Presence isn't plain to you, it doesn't mean that He's left you; it just means He's guarding you.

Your journey to self-discovery will equip and empower you for your race. You have one last lap to go. Your witnesses are still cheering for you. Keep running. Your fans are waiting for you to cross the finish line. *So what* if you come in last place? The fans are still cheering for you. You still have the stamina to make it, because God is with you! How do you think you've made it this far? Surely, you didn't make it on your own. In fact, you would've given up a long time ago if that were the case. Instead, God gave you the power to persevere. One last lap to go and you'll be victorious. One last lap and you find out what you are made of. One last lap and you'll be able to say, "I hung in there until the end! I did it! I've finished my race!"

Chapter 12

Crossing the Finish Line

"When I found that I had crossed that line [the Mason-Dixon Line], I looked at my hands to see if I was the same person. There was such a glory over everything; the sun came like gold through the trees, and over the fields, and I felt like I was in Heaven."

—Harriet Tubman

the finish line - *noun.* a line indicating the location of the finish of a race.

O nce you cross that finish line, you join the club. You've earned your membership to an elite group of individuals. Whether you've finished first, last, or somewhere in the middle, you belong to this collection of accomplished people. Everything that follows is an extension of your victory. You've done it! In between the starting line and the finishing line, while struggling and persevering, you transformed — you became a contender.

The finish line is the beginning of yet another race. Life is a sequence of races, a series of starting and finishing lines. With the start of the next race, though, you will be stronger, faster, and more determined. You will find yourself standing at many more starting lines, beginning many more races. And for these acts of inauguration, for these decisions to participate in life's race, you will be granted hope. Standing at a starting line, any starting line, gives you permission to hope. Simply garnering the courage to begin a task, to stand at its starting line, instills the precious notion of optimism. This optimism will drive you from race to race and will eventually convert into expectation. Soon you will *expect* success.

Crossing the starting line may be a noteworthy act of courage, but crossing the finish line is a beautiful act of faith. Faith, if you don't know it, is one of humanity's most powerful emotions. Faith is the wind which propels us forward when we are tired and weary and want nothing more than to retreat. Faith is the mighty emotion that conquers fear. Faith is the emotion that grants us victory over our past, over the demons in our souls, and over all of those voices that tell us what we can and cannot be.

If standing at the starting line gives you permission to dream, crossing the finish line gives you permission to plan. Crossing the finish line allows you to design your next success, and to plan for the realization of your next dream. The last step of the race is the first step of the rest of your life.

Hold On!

I'm reminded of a time when I was having a conversation on the phone with a friend of mine, Mrs. Jenkins, who had recently overcome many obstacles in her life. She had suffered a devastating divorce which could have left her financially crippled with no means of caring for her family. Her ex-husband, who was an undercover millionaire, had maneuvered a way to hide his funds and pay her nothing after fifteen years of marriage. With nothing left, she put everything in God's Hands. She surrendered to His Will. Then she went on a mission to reclaim her life, her self-esteem, and her happiness. Now all she needed was the comfort of knowing she was divorced. After a long, hard-fought, six-year court battle, she said to the judge, "Your honor, I'm sick and tired of all of this. I don't want anything. Just give me my divorce!" The judge looked confused for a moment by what seemed an obtuse request, but he granted her wish. She stumbled out of the courtroom in despair, with no sign of hope, no financial obligation from her ex-husband, no right to the home they had built together, nothing. All she had was God's Will, which consistently said to her, "Hold on." Despite being raised in a poverty-stricken community, Mrs. Jenkins' goals were enormous. She had to move out of her home and into an apartment, but she remained inspired. She managed to turn her life around within two years of her divorce. She had worked in someone else's shop for more than twenty years as a beautician, but on her road to recovery, she began to acknowledge her dream of one day opening up her own hair salon.

Of course, she met many obstacles on that journey. At first there was no money to finance her dream. A deal gone bad almost left her in shambles. But by following God's Will ("Hold on" it said), she finally saw her dream come true and opened up an elegant hair salon with a stable staff. She bought a town-house, which was ten times better than the home she'd lost. Later, she purchased her dream home, a luxurious single-family home in a suburban community, three-times better and larger than her town home. She then remarried an honorable and devoted gentleman who added even more happiness to her life.

In profound words of faith, she told me, "Michael, this is not the end to my beginning...this is the beginning of my beginning." She knew more blessings were in store.

It appears that Mrs. Jenkins possessed the power and the potency of the lightening bug. What makes the lightning bug glow with its brilliant-green iridescence is a substance called auto-luminescent protein. In other words, the bug doesn't need outside light to glow. It glows from within itself, with its own internal light.

It's a creation of God. Therefore, it glows in the presence *and* absence of other lightning bugs, just as you should glow in the presence and in the absence of your friends and family members. The lightning bug doesn't need any external support in order to turn on its inner light for everyone to see, and nei-ther do you. It already has that capability in its biological make-up, and so do you. You must adopt the lightning-bug theory if you expect to finish your race in life. And when you do, make sure you take off flying and illuminate yourself, so others can see and appreciate your light.

If you believe you can, you will. No matter what goal you set for yourself, always keep an image of the finish line in sight, and don't stop until you get there.

By finishing what you start, you'll find that the easiest thing is doing it; the hardest thing is believing you could. Many people fail because they don't believe in themselves. Once you believe that nothing in the world can stop you from achieving your goals — except you — nothing in the world can impede your destiny. Not trusting God and not believing in my ability to finish school hindered me, just as a lack of faith and self-confidence prevents many people from reaching their goals.

What you do now is up to you. You've seen what you're capable of. If you've stuck with the training program, you've seen yourself filled with joy and blinded by frustration. You've overcome your fears. You've been humbled by both the strength and the fragility of your body. You've found what you thought were your limits, and you have gone beyond them.

You've also learned that what stops most of us from achieving our dreams — as athletes and as people — are the confines of our imaginations. We can never be more than we imagine we can be. And as long as we are restricted by our imaginations, we are forever bound to our pasts and blinded to our futures.

Your limits now lie behind you. By taking that final step across the finish line, you have freed yourself from all of the things you ever thought you knew about yourself. By crossing the finish line, you have taken the very first step on the divine track to your life. Are you ready? Sure you are! Get up and win that race!

I leave you with an anonymous poem which continues to inspire me in my race in life. I hope it does the same for you.

The Race

Whenever I start to hang my head in front of failure's face,
my downward fall is broken by the memory of a race.

A children's race, young boys, young men; how I remember
well, excitement, sure, but also fear, it wasn't hard to tell.

They all lined up so full of hope, each thought to win that race
or tie for first, or if not that, at least take second place.

Their parents watched from off the side, each cheering for
their son, and each boy hoped to show his folks that he would
be the one.

The whistle blew and off they flew, like chariots of fire,
to win, to be the hero there, was each young boy's desire.

One boy in particular, whose dad was in the crowd, was
running in the lead and thought "My dad will be so proud."

But as he speeded down the field and crossed a shallow dip,
the little boy who thought he'd win, lost his step and slipped.

Trying hard to catch himself, his arms flew everyplace,
and midst the laughter of the crowd he fell flat on his face.

214

As he fell, his hope fell too; he couldn't win it now.
Humiliated, he just wished to disappear somehow.
But as he fell his dad stood up and showed his anxious face,
which to the boy so clearly said, "Get up and win that race!"

He quickly rose, no damage done, behind a bit that's all,
and ran with all his mind and might to make up for his fall.
So anxious to restore himself, to catch up and to win,
his mind went faster than his legs. He slipped and fell again.

He wished that he had quit before with only one disgrace.
"I'm hopeless as a runner now, I shouldn't try to race."
But through the laughing crowd he searched and found his
father's face with a steady look that said again,
"Get up and win that race!"

So he jumped up to try again, ten yards behind the last.
"If I'm to gain those yards," he thought, "I've got to run real fast!"
Exceeding everything he had, he regained eight, then ten. . .
but trying hard to catch the lead, he slipped and fell again.

Defeat! He lay there silently. A tear dropped from his eye.
"There's no sense running anymore! Three strikes I'm out!
Why try?
I've lost, so what's the use?" he thought. "I'll live with my
disgrace."
But then he thought about his dad, who soon he'd have to face.

"Get up," an echo sounded low, "you haven't lost at all,
for all you have to do to win is rise each time you fall.

Get up!" the echo urged him on, "Get up and take your place!
You were not meant for failure here! Get up and win that race!"

So, up he rose to run once more, refusing to forfeit,
and he resolved that win or lose, at least he wouldn't quit.
So far behind the others now, the most he'd ever been,
still he gave it all he had and ran like he could win.

Three times he'd fallen stumbling, three times he rose again.
Too far behind to hope to win, he still ran to the end.
They cheered another boy who crossed the line and won first
place, head high and proud and happy — no falling, no disgrace.

But, when the fallen youngster crossed the line, in last place,
the crowd gave him a greater cheer for finishing the race.
And even though he came in last with head bowed low, unproud,
you would have thought he'd won the race, to listen to the crowd.

And to his dad he sadly said, "I didn't do so well."
"To me, you won," his father said. "You rose each time you fell."
And now when things seem dark and bleak and difficult to face,
the memory of that little boy helps me in my own race.

For all of life is like that race, with ups and downs and all.
And all you have to do to win is rise each time you fall.
And when depression and despair shout loudly in my face,
another voice within me says, "Get up and win that race!"

About the Author

Michael Miller delivers powerful messages that penetrate the minds of urban youth worldwide. His messages are clear and simple, yet provocative and well grounded. As one of the nation's most prolific and dynamic speakers, he motivates thousands of students and adult learners, and travels extensively across the country conducting lectures, workshops, and professional development training sessions. This scholar, motivational speaker, author, and lecturer is acclaimed by many media outlets as "one of the future leaders of tomorrow."

In a matter of three years, he obtained his GED, A.A. degree, and a B.A. degree from Morehouse College and set a national record as the first person ever to do so.

In 2000, Miller was honored by Morehouse College as a *Beating the Odds* scholar. He was recognized for his efforts as a single parent, full-time student, and as a dedicated father with up to $100, 000 to complete his matriculation through the benevolence of Oprah Winfrey. Michael Miller later received his Masters of Science in Psychology and his Doctorate degree in Urban Educational Leadership. He has received countless awards, including the Dr. Martin Luther King Jr. *Footsteps Award*, *Academic Achievement of the Year*, and *Father of the Year*. He was featured in the *Who's Who Among Students In America*. Above all, he was named Motivational Speaker and Writer of the Year for 2000-2003 by the *Speakers Bureau of America*.

Michael Miller has not forgotten his roots: he continues to give back to his Baltimore community. He is the Founder and President of the *O.D.D.S. Foundation,* through which students are mentored and awarded scholarships to attend college to further their education. Through his leadership, over thirty new youth and adult literacy scholarships and programs have been established nationwide. As the US Ambassador for Adult Education, Miller is a beacon of hope who travels extensively empowering young people that "It doesn't matter where you start, what counts is where you decide to finish."

Order Form

ORDER NOW

Name_____

Company Name_____

Address_____

City:_____State:_____Zip:_____

Telephone: (___) _____Email:_____

Please send me _____copies of **A Promise to Persevere**

Price	**Shipping**:	**Total**
$15.99	$3.50 per book	$19.49

Sales Tax: Add 5% to books shipped to Maryland addresses.

Check____ Money Order____ Cashiers Check_____

Total enclosed: $_____

Make payable and send to:
Empowerment Press Publishing Company
P.O. Box 794
Ellicott City, MD 21041-794
Phone: 1-800-818-6010

Please allow 7 days for delivery.

***

Books are available at special discounts for bulk purchases, sales promotion, fundraising or educational purposes.

For more information write to:
Empowerment Press Publishing Company
PO Box 794,
Ellicott City, MD 21041-794, USA
Phone: 1-800-818-6010
Or visit our website at www.apromisetopersevere.com

Notes

Notes

Notes

Notes